*The Cambridge Introduction to*
## Jacques Derrida

Few thinkers of the latter half of the twentieth century have so profoundly and radically transformed our understanding of writing and literature as Jacques Derrida (1930–2004). Derridian deconstruction remains one of the most powerful intellectual movements of the present century, and Derrida's own innovative writings on literature and philosophy are crucially relevant for any understanding of the future of literature and literary criticism today. Derrida's own manner of writing is complex and challenging and has often been misrepresented or misunderstood. In this book, Leslie Hill provides an accessible introduction to Derrida's writings on literature which presupposes no prior knowledge of Derrida's work. He explores in detail Derrida's relationship to literary theory and criticism, and offers close readings of some of Derrida's best known essays. This introduction will help those coming to Derrida's work for the first time, and suggests further directions to take in studying this hugely influential thinker.

Leslie Hill is Professor of French Studies at the University of Warwick.

# Cambridge Introductions to Literature

This series is designed to introduce students to key topics and authors. Accessible and lively, these introductions will also appeal to readers who want to broaden their understanding of the books and authors they enjoy.

- Ideal for students, teachers, and lecturers
- Concise, yet packed with essential information
- Key suggestions for further reading

**Titles in this series:**

# The Cambridge Introduction to
# Jacques Derrida

LESLIE HILL

CAMBRIDGE
UNIVERSITY PRESS

CAMBRIDGE UNIVERSITY PRESS
Cambridge, New York, Melbourne, Madrid, Cape Town, Singapore, São Paulo

Cambridge University Press
The Edinburgh Building, Cambridge CB2 8RU, UK

Published in the United States of America by Cambridge University Press, New York

www.cambridge.org
Information on this title: www.cambridge.org/9780521682817

First published 2007

Printed in the United Kingdom at the University Press, Cambridge

*A catalogue record for this publication is available from the British Library*

ISBN 978-0-521-86416-9 hardback
ISBN 978-0-521-68281-7 paperback

# Contents

# Preface

The implications, range, and sheer volume of the work of Jacques Derrida are huge. They far exceed by any calculation what it is possible to discuss adequately in a modest introductory volume of this kind. For this, and other reasons, I have limited myself to only one of the multiple, variegated threads running through Derrida's writing: his reading of that body of texts known to audiences the world over as 'literature'. This book, then, is addressed primarily, though I hope not exclusively, to students of literature with an interest in literary theory, and, more generally, to readers wishing to know more about the already lengthy, infinite conversation between literature and philosophy as it is both interrupted and prolonged in Derrida's work.

Derrida, as many will be aware, places demands on his readers. This is not only because his writing is dense and at times elliptical; not only because it presupposes at least a degree of familiarity with the main tenets of some of the key texts in the Western philosophical tradition, from Plato, Kant, and Hegel to Husserl, Freud, and Heidegger; not only because his work is deeply informed by a particular philosophical, intellectual, and literary context that has its own complex and specific history, aspects of which may be unfamiliar to Derrida's non-francophone readership; and not only because it exploits the resources of French language and idiom in ways that border at times on the untranslatable. All this is true. But there is also more: it is that his work challenges readers to rethink many inherited assumptions, up to and including those governing the basis on which thought, writing, language occur at all.

It was no doubt inevitable that the boldness and radicalism of Derrida's enterprise would meet with resistance, not to say incomprehension and mis-representation. Readers new to Derrida should however remember, contrary to what is sometimes alleged, that from the very outset Derrida was an impla-cable opponent of irrationalism and obscurantism in all its many forms, and a writer who took seriously his responsibilities as a thinker, teacher, and public intellectual. Any who know his work well will agree: when it is a matter of rigorous argument, few writers are as lucid, consistent, exacting, scrupulous, or discriminating as Derrida.

Derrida's reputation, no doubt, is forever indissociable from a word he first coined, then made famous, and in the end accepted reluctantly as a possible description of his work: deconstruction. Deconstruction, like the devil, is all in the detail. In this book, it is therefore not solely with the strategic imperatives of Derrida's thinking that I shall be concerned, but also with much of the specific detail of his readings of literary and other texts. For whoever agrees to present Derrida's work is in a quandary. First, some may wonder, is there any need for an introductory book at all? After all, the most effective introduction to Derrida's work already exists: it is that work itself, which the reader is hereby enjoined simply to read, in as sustained a manner as possible. Some of that work, admittedly, can be difficult. An introductory volume such as this does, then, have a part to play. But in seeking to make Derrida more accessible, is it better to focus on the larger picture, or on the smaller, to confine oneself to always questionable paraphrase, or to enter into the intricate, but all the more revealing detail of individual texts?

Unable to reconcile itself unreservedly, in the end, to either solution, this book has sought to chart a middle course, believing in the end that accessibility, truth, and fidelity each matter in a project of this kind, and that what best assists readers new to Derrida – and all readers, at one point or another, are new to Derrida – is not a digested read nor a digested digest, but a measure of patient preliminary engagement not with the urban myth of deconstruction, whatever the word is taken to mean, but with the writing signed Jacques Derrida in so far as it constitutes one of the essential events in the history of modern thought.

Fidelity, true enough, is impossible, and infidelity inevitable: happily and unhappily. One of the tasks of this book, no doubt, will have been to demonstrate the inescapability of the dilemma, safe only in the knowledge that there is no alternative but to accept and rejoice in it, while acknowledging too the responsibility it implies.

I should like here to record my thanks to colleagues at the University of Warwick who have given me invaluable support in enabling me to complete this book. I am also indebted to many students, in Philosophy and Literature, Philosophy, French Studies, and English Studies at the University, who, over the last decade, have contributed more than they may realise to the pages that follow.

I should like, finally, to dedicate this book to Susie and Juliet: that they too may begin to understand.

# Abbreviations

The principal texts by Jacques Derrida to which I refer in the course of this book are identified by the following abbreviations. Where two sets of page numbers are given, the first refer to Derrida's original French text (even when, as in some cases, this appeared in print after the corresponding English translation), and the second to the current English-language edition of the text. For accuracy, consistency, or sometimes clarity, I have here and there modified these translations. Where no English version is currently available, translations given are my own.

A    *Acts of Literature*, edited by Derek Attridge, London, Routledge, 1992.

AA   with Antoine Spire, *Au-delà des apparences*, Latresne, Editions Le Bord de l'eau, 2002.

AT   *D'un ton apocalyptique adopté naguère en philosophie*, Paris, Galilée, 1983; 'On A Newly Arisen Apocalyptic Tone in Philosophy', translated by John Leavey, Jr, in *Raising the Tone of Philosophy*, edited by Peter Fenves, Baltimore, The Johns Hopkins University Press, 1993, 117–71.

AV   *Apprendre à vivre enfin*, Paris, Galilée, 2005.

BB   *A Derrida Reader: Between the Blinds*, edited by Peggy Kamuf, New York, Columbia University Press, 1991.

C    with Catherine Malabou, *La Contre-allée*, Paris, La Quinzaine littéraire, 1999; *Counterpath: Traveling With Jacques Derrida*, translated by David Wills, Stanford, Stanford University Press, 2004.

D    *La Dissémination*, Paris, Seuil, 1972; *Dissemination*, translated by Barbara Johnson, Chicago, University of Chicago Press, 1981.

DC   'Living On', translated by James Hulbert, in Harold Bloom et al., *Deconstruction and Criticism*, London, Routledge, 1979, 75–176.

DFT  Maurice Blanchot/Jacques Derrida, *The Instant of My Death / Demeure: Fiction and Testimony*, translated by Elizabeth Rottenberg, Stanford, Stanford University Press, 2000.

DN    *Deconstruction in a Nutshell: A Conversation with Jacques Derrida*,
      edited with a commentary by John D. Caputo, New York, Fordham
      University Press, 1997.

DP    *Du droit à la philosophie*, Paris, Galilée, 1990; *Who's Afraid of
      Philosophy?: Right to Philosophy*, translated by Jan Plug, Stanford,
      Stanford University Press, 2002.

DT    'Des Tours de Babel', *Difference in Translation*, edited by Joseph
      F. Graham, Ithaca, Cornell University Press, 1985, 165–207

E     *Eperons*, Paris, Flammarion, 1978; *Spurs*, translated by Barbara
      Harlow, Chicago, University of Chicago Press, 1979.

G     *De la grammatologie*, Paris, Minuit, 1967; *Of Grammatology*,
      corrected edition, translated by Gayatri Chakravorty Spivak,
      Baltimore, Johns Hopkins University Press (1976), 1997.

Gl    *Glas*, Paris, Galilée, 1974; *Glas*, translated by John P. Leavey, Jnr and
      Richard Rand, Lincoln, University of Nebraska Press, 1986.
      References to the left- or right-hand columns of Derrida's text are
      indicated by the use of *a* or *b* respectively.

HF    'Interview with Jacques Derrida', *Heidegger en France*, edited by
      Dominique Janicaud, 2 vols., Vol. II, Paris, Albin Michel, 2001,
      89–126.

L     *Limited Inc*, edited by Gerald Graff, introduced and translated by
      Elisabeth Weber, Paris, Galilée, 1990; *Limited Inc*, edited by Gerald
      Graff, Evanston, Ill., Northwestern University Press, 1988.

M     *Marges: de la philosophie*, Paris, Minuit, 1972; *Margins of Philosophy*,
      translated by Alan Bass, Chicago, University of Chicago Press, 1982.

MM    *Mémoires pour Paul de Man*, Paris, Galilée, 1988; *Memoires for Paul
      de Man*, translated by Cecile Lindsay, Jonathan Culler, Eduardo
      Cadava, and Peggy Kamuf, New York, Columbia University Press,
      revised edition, 1989.

MO    *Le Monolinguisme de l'autre, ou la prothèse d'origine*, Paris, Galilée,
      1996; *Monolingualism of the Other; or, The Prosthesis of Origin*,
      translated by Patrick Mensah, Stanford, Stanford University Press,
      1998.

MS    *Marx & Sons*, Paris, P.U.F.-Galilée, 2002; 'Marx & Sons', translated
      by G. M. Goshgarian, in *Ghostly Demarcations*, edited by Michael
      Sprinker, London, Verso, 1999, 213–69.

N     *Negotiations: Interventions and Interviews, 1971–2001*, edited and
      translated by Elizabeth Rottenberg, Stanford, Stanford University
      Press, 2002.

OCC      'Signé l'ami d'un "ami de la Chine"', in *Aux origines de la Chine contemporaine: en hommage à Lucien Bianco*, edited by Marie-Claire Bergère, Paris, L'Harmattan, 2002, i–xv.

OG      Edmund Husserl, *L'Origine de la géométrie*, translated and introduced by Jacques Derrida, Paris, P.U.F., 1962; *Edmund Husserl's Origin of Geometry: An Introduction*, translated by John P. Leavey, Jr, New York, Harvester Press, 1978.

OH      *L'Autre Cap*, Paris, Minuit, 1991; *The Other Heading*, translated by Pascale-Anne Brault and Michael B. Naas, Bloomington, Indiana University Press, 1992.

P      *Parages*, Paris, Galilée (1986), 2003.

Pa      *Passions*, Paris, Galilée, 1993; 'Passions', in *On the Name*, edited by Thomas Dutoit, translated by David Wood, John P. Leavey, Jr, and Ian McLeod, Stanford, Stanford University Press, 1995.

PC      *La Carte postale*, Paris, Aubier-Flammarion, 1980; *The Post Card*, translated by Alan Bass, Chicago, University of Chicago Press, 1987.

PG      *Le Problème de la genèse dans la philosophie de Husserl*, Paris, P.U.F., 1990; *The Problem of Genesis in Husserl's Philosophy*, translated by Marian Hobson, Chicago, University of Chicago Press, 2003.

PM      *Papier machine*, Paris, Galilée, 2001.

Po      *Positions*, Paris, Minuit, 1972; *Positions*, translated by Alan Bass, London, The Athlone Press, 1981.

Pr      'Préjugés: devant la loi', in *La Faculté de juger*, Paris, Minuit, 1985, 87–139.

PS      *Points de suspension*, Paris, Galilée, 1992; *Points . . ., Interviews 1974–1994*, translated by Peggy Kamuf and others, Stanford, Stanford University Press, 1995.

PSJ      'Two Words for Joyce', translated by Geoff Bennington, in *Post-Structuralist Joyce*, edited by Derek Attridge and Daniel Ferrer, Cambridge, Cambridge University Press, 1984, 145–59.

Psy      *Psyché: inventions de l'autre*, Paris, Galilée, 1987.

R      *Résistances de la psychanalyse*, Paris, Galilée, 1996; *Resistances of Psychoanalysis*, translated by Peggy Kamuf, Pascale-Anne Brault, and Michael Naas, Stanford, Stanford University Press, 1998.

RD      'Jacques n'a voulu . . .', *Rue Descartes*, 48, April 2005, 6–7.

S      *Signéponge*, Paris, Seuil, 1988; *Signéponge/Signsponge*, translated by Richard Rand, New York, Columbia University Press, 1984.

SM      *Spectres de Marx*, Paris, Galilée, 1993; *Specters of Marx*, translated by Peggy Kamuf, London, Routledge, 1994.

SP        *Sur parole: instantanés philosophiques*, La Tour d'Aigues, éditions de
          l'Aube, 1999.
TM        with Safaa Fathy, *Tourner les mots: au bord d'un film*, Paris, Galilée,
          2000.
TP        *La Vérité en peinture*, Paris, Flammarion, 1974; *The Truth in
          Painting*, translated by Geoff Bennington and Ian McLeod, Chicago,
          Chicago University Press, 1987.
TS        with Maurizio Ferraris, *A Taste for the Secret*, translated by Giacomo
          Donis, edited by Giacomo Donis and David Webb, Cambridge,
          Polity, 2001.
TT        'The Time of a Thesis: Punctuations', translated by Kathleen
          McLaughlin, in *Philosophy in France Today*, edited by Alan
          Montefiore, Cambridge, Cambridge University Press, 1983.
UG        *Ulysse gramophone*, Paris, Galilée, 1987.
WD        *L'Ecriture et la différence*, Paris, Seuil, 1967; *Writing and Différence*,
          translated by Alan Bass, London, Routledge, 1978.
WT        with Elisabeth Roudinesco, *De quoi demain . . .* , Paris, Flammarion:
          Champs, 2001; *For What Tomorrow: A Dialogue*, translated by Jeff
          Fort, Stanford, Stanford University Press, 2004.

# Chapter 1

# Life

Few philosophers, in the latter half of the twentieth century, so profoundly and radically transformed our understanding of writing, reading, texts, and textuality as Jacques Derrida. The scope of Derrida's thinking is prodigious. It explores with extraordinary inventiveness and originality some of the most pressing practical and theoretical challenges of recent times, in philosophy, politics, ethics, literary theory, criticism, psychoanalysis, legal theory, and much else besides; it articulates a fresh and rigorous account of the complex cultural, philosophical, and religious legacy of the West, its achievements and its silences, its exclusions and unfulfilled promises; and it develops a new style of reading scrupulously adjusted to the general implications and intricate singularity of philosophical and literary texts, to their relevance within the history of thought and the question of their enduring but always fragile future. The scale of Derrida's published output is similarly imposing. In the course of an intellectual career spanning five decades, he published well in excess of 100 volumes, including sustained monographs on key themes or topics, a wealth of lecture, seminar, and conference presentations brought together in a series of wide-ranging collections of essays, many other more localised interventions, including a stream of interviews, prefaces, prepared and unprepared responses to different audiences and to other thinkers, not to mention numerous other autobiographical or other writings impossible to categorise in conventional terms. And though Derrida wrote almost exclusively in his native French, he soon acquired a worldwide reputation and saw his work translated into English, Spanish, Portuguese, Italian, German, Greek, Russian, Czech, Hungarian, Polish, Bulgarian, Arabic, Japanese, and many other languages too.[1]

Derrida's beginnings were, in fact, relatively modest. He was born Jackie Derrida on 15 July 1930 in El-Biar, a district on the south side of Algiers, during the period of French colonial rule. His father, Aimé Derrida, a commercial traveller for a wines-and-spirits firm, and his mother, Georgette Safar, were both Jews, whose forebears, arriving from Spain, had lived in Algeria since pre-colonial times, i.e. before the annexation of the country by the French in 1830. This meant that they became eligible for French citizenship only as a result of the Crémieux decree enacted in 1870, which naturalised *en bloc* all Jews born in Algeria.[2] As far as the Jewish population in Algeria was concerned, which numbered some 110,127 people according to the 1931 census, not to mention Derrida's own immediate family, this award of French citizenship was however short-lived, for one of the first measures introduced by the collaborationist Vichy government in October 1940 was the abrogation of the *décret Crémieux*.[3] Already Vichy itself was keen to outdo even Hitler in the extent of its anti-semitic legislation, and the authorities in Algeria proved more eager still, extending to primary and secondary schools the severe anti-Jewish quotas imposed by Vichy, which meant that from June 1942 onwards, Derrida, aged 11 at the time, like many of his Jewish fellow students, found himself forcibly excluded from state education (*PC*, 97; 87–8; *MO*, 34–7; 16–18). Until the following spring, he attended instead – at least in name, since in reality he seems to have been persistently absent – the unofficial secondary school set up with the help of Jewish teachers who had similarly been dismissed by the authorities. In November 1942, when the Allied American and British forces landed in Algeria, it seemed as though things would quickly improve, but the new French regime, comprising many anti-semitic elements who had previously supported Vichy, was markedly slow in reversing the situation, with the governor-general, Marcel Peyrouton, a former Vichy interior minister, arguing that to reinstate the Crémieux decree would encourage similar demands on the part of the disenfranchised majority Muslim population.[4] It was not until the Autumn of 1943 that Jewish students were allowed to rejoin mainstream secondary education.

The experience at the time for Derrida, he later remarked, was both puzzling and brutal. It left him with a deep suspicion of any kind of communitarian politics based on racial, ethnic, or religious identification, and translated too into an abiding reticence to speak in the first person plural, as *we* or part of an *us*, in the name of this or that larger community, even including that Jewish community of which he was nominally a member (*AV*, 40–7). It also served to alienate Derrida from the educational institution in general, and it is not surprising that during his adolescent years Derrida's academic record was that of a disaffected, often unhappy student, one of whose ambitions, even as he had begun to take an interest in Rousseau, Gide, and Nietzsche (*SP*, 16–17), was to be a professional footballer, or even perhaps an actor: an early photograph, shown in Safaa Fathy's documentary *D'ailleurs, Derrida* (*Derrida's Elsewhere*) depicts him at the age of fifteen, with bow-and-arrow, dressed as Tarzan (*TM*, 96–7)!

By the end of the 1940s, however, things began to change. After successfully passing his *baccalauréat* at the second attempt in June 1948, Derrida began to take a more active academic interest in literature and philosophy. At the age of nineteen, this took him for the very first time out of his native Algiers to Paris. Before then, his travelling had been limited to accompanying his father by car on his rounds, which rarely extended beyond 200 kilometres from the family home (*C*, 31, 37; 27, 32). If the 1942 Allied invasion had been the first landing to alter the course of his life, Derrida later remarked, so his landing in Marseille en route to Paris was the second (*TM*, 95–6). He did not settle easily at first in the capital. But in 1952 he eventually gained admission to the prestigious elite institution of the Ecole normale supérieure, through which had passed, in earlier decades, some of the most prominent philosophical and literary figures of the age, from Henri Bergson to Jean-Paul Sartre.

At the Ecole normale Derrida encountered as teachers or fellow students many who would soon become leading figures in their own right: the Marxist philosopher Louis Althusser, who was already an important member of the Ecole normale teaching staff, the philosopher and historian Michel Foucault, who also taught Derrida for a time, the sociologist Pierre Bourdieu, the philosopher of aesthetics Louis Marin, the Sinologist Lucien Bianco, and the literary critic and theorist Gérard Genette. This was a remarkably creative generation who collectively, within twenty years or so, radically changed the whole philosophical and theoretical landscape both in France and elsewhere; in the 1980s and 1990s it would increasingly fall to Derrida to act as a standard-bearer for what had been achieved. So it was that he came to be responsible for numerous obituaries and eulogies: for such friends and colleagues as Foucault, Marin, and Althusser, and other influential thinkers of the period as Roland Barthes, Paul De Man, Gilles Deleuze, and Jean-François Lyotard. Increasingly, towards the end of his own life, it was not surprising that Derrida often thought of himself, he said, as something of a survivor.[5]

In 1954 while at the Ecole normale, Derrida completed a first lengthy dissertation, which was not published till 1990, entitled *Le Problème de la genèse dans la philosophie de Husserl* (*The Problem of Genesis in Husserl's Philosophy*), in which Derrida dealt with some of the difficulties and tensions existing in the thought of Edmund Husserl (1859–1938), the founder and architect of modern phenomenology. Two years later, having successfully obtained the highly competitive advanced teaching qualification, the *agrégation*, and on the pretext of pursuing his research on Husserl, Derrida travelled to the United States where he spent a year as a visiting student at Harvard in what was to be, Derrida remarked, the third significant landfall in his career. On his return to France in 1957, Derrida submitted the title for a doctoral thesis closely related to his work on Husserl. But for a variety of personal, political, and institutional reasons the project was never completed, and Derrida was finally awarded a doctorate only in 1980 on the basis of his published work. In his thesis defence, while retracing his intellectual itinerary, he took the opportunity to explain, as we shall see, why it was that his thinking, for essential reasons, had never proven reducible to a *thesis* (*DP*, 439–59; *TT*, 34–50).

In 1957, before proceeding further in his academic career, along with all other French males of arms-bearing age, Derrida was obliged to carry out compulsory military service, which he did in a non-military setting, teaching in a primary school in Algeria for the next two years. These were turbulent times in the country. The war for Algerian independence begun in 1954 was slowly reaching a decisive climax, and soon after, under the April 1962 Evian accords, culminated in France's final withdrawal from the country, which it had admittedly never viewed as a colony but as a natural extension of its own territory. Many settlers of French descent left for the mainland, as did others, like Derrida's own family, whose primary allegiance was to French language and culture and to the universalism of the French Republic, which had distinguished itself long ago, unlike the Vichy State, by its emancipation of the Jews. In 1959 Derrida similarly returned to Paris, where his academic and intellectual career now began in earnest. After five years spent teaching at the Sorbonne, he took a position at the Ecole normale supérieure where he remained for the next twenty years, notwithstanding his international celebrity, in the surprisingly modest role of *maître-assistant* or lecturer.

By the end of the decade, Derrida had established himself as a powerful new voice and publishing presence, bringing out in 1967 no fewer than three separate volumes: *La Voix et le phénomène* (*Speech and Phenomena*, translated 1973), *De la grammatologie* (*Of Grammatology*, translated 1976); *L'Ecriture et la différence* (*Writing and Difference*, translated 1978), followed, five years later, in 1972, by three more, equally substantial books: *La Dissémination* (*Dissemination*, translated 1981), *Marges de la philosophie* (*Margins of Philosophy*, translated 1982), and *Positions* (*Positions*, translated 1981). These respective dates for original French and subsequent English publication are not insignificant; they are a useful measure of Derrida's increasing prominence in the English-speaking world throughout the 1980s and 1990s. For while *De la grammatologie*, like *La Dissémination*, had to wait almost a decade before being translated, a much later book, *Specters of Marx*, first published in French in 1993, admittedly drawing on material presented in English at a conference in California some months before, was already available in translation the following year. *Monolingualism of the Other* and *Resistances of Psychoanalysis*, both published in French in 1996, were likewise quickly translated, appearing in English only two years later.

In his early books of 1967 and 1972, Derrida ranged widely over the work of several canonic and non-canonic philosophical and literary figures, from Plato,

Hegel, Husserl, Heidegger, Freud, Saussure, Lévi-Strauss, Foucault, and Levinas on the one hand, to Rousseau, Mallarmé, Artaud, Bataille, Jabès, and Sollers on the other, bringing these seemingly disparate philosophical and literary writings into close critical proximity, not in order to dismiss or underplay the complex differences between the literary and the philosophical, but rather to examine their shared implication in questions of writing, language, and style. And if in his early work he addressed the question of writing now in philosophical works, now in literary texts, in 1974 Derrida went a step further in his most provocative and challenging book yet, *Glas* (*Glas*, translated 1986), which was in the form of a double reading spread across parallel columns of selected works by G. W. F. Hegel, the imperious nineteenth-century philosopher of Absolute Knowledge, and the fiction and plays of one of the twentieth century's most avowedly marginal authors, the self-confessed 'coward, traitor, thief, and queer',[6] Jean Genet. What was at stake here was not the subordination of literature to philosophy or philosophy to literature, as some have hastily concluded, but an exploration of what it was that took place *between* the so-called philosophical and the so-called literary, which was to be the central focus of much of Derrida's thinking in the years to come.

Following in the wake of the strikes and demonstrations of May 1968, the 1970s in France, as far as the education system was concerned, were a period of fierce polarisation on the part of both left and right, and though Derrida had limited enthusiasm for the events of May themselves, he took a leading role in the subsequent campaign to defend philosophy as a discipline against the political attacks mounted against it by successive conservative administrations. There was an important need, in Derrida's eyes, both to rethink the relationship between philosophy and the institution of the university and to reinvent the institutional basis for the teaching of philosophy at both secondary and university level. These concerns on Derrida's part were immediate but also long-lasting, and gave rise, from 1974 onwards, to his involvement in the Greph (Groupe de recherches sur l'enseignement philosophique or Philosophy Teaching Research Group), and in 1983 to the founding of the Collège international de philosophie, that mobile interdisciplinary coalition that in recent decades has played a key role in France as a platform for innovative thinking in philosophy and in the humanities.

In the mid-1970s, too, together with his colleagues Sarah Kofman, Philippe Lacoue-Labarthe, and Jean-Luc Nancy, Derrida was instrumental in launching, first with Aubier-Flammarion, then with the newly revived Editions Galilée, a book series called 'La Philosophie en effet' (roughly translatable as 'Philosophy in deed'), which served as an important outlet for new approaches in the discipline. These initiatives were not restricted to mainland France. In 1981, with colleagues from other countries, Derrida helped set up the Jan Hus Association to support dissident or persecuted intellectuals in Communist Czechoslovakia. It was during a visit to Prague to speak at a clandestine seminar that Derrida was arrested and imprisoned on suspicion of drug trafficking, only to be released (and deported) shortly after as a result of the direct intervention of François Mitterrand, the newly elected French president.

During the 1970s Derrida's reputation took on a decisively international character. By 1976, for instance, *De la grammatologie* was now available in Italian, Spanish, Japanese, Portuguese, as well as English translation, and this led to an increasing number of invitations abroad, with Derrida becoming a frequent visitor to the United States, giving lectures and seminars at Johns Hopkins, then at Yale, and then at the University of California, Irvine, and other institutions too. In 1979 his growing prominence on the English-speaking stage found expression in the book *Deconstruction and Criticism*, co-authored with Harold Bloom, Paul de Man, Geoffrey Hartman, and J. Hillis Miller, the title of which had the unfortunate effect of identifying Derrida's work with a label he had never claimed as such, and would always find reductive, and creating for some readers at least the misleading impression that his work was simply a kind of literary criticism applied to philosophical texts.

Much debate, controversy, and polemic ensued, particularly in the English-speaking world, much of it ill-informed, and sad confirmation of the fact that it is sometimes easier for professional commentators not to understand what they are (or, more likely, are not) reading. Derrida's enthusiasm remained however undimmed. He carried on tirelessly explaining, developing, and reinventing his thinking in a wide range of different settings, languages, and forums, displaying an unfailing commitment to his responsibilities as thinker, teacher, and engaged intellectual. He campaigned against apartheid, against racism in all its forms, against the assault of the French state on those it deemed to be illegal immigrants, against the death penalty, against state terrorism, whatever its provenance. He remained throughout deeply critical, too, of the grossly simplifying tendencies characteristic of highly mediatised, globalised contemporary Western societies, and deploying his formidable intellectual resources in the effort to understand the threat to democracy of what, since the end of the twentieth century, has come to be known as the new world order.

Derrida's intellectual itinerary displays many unreconciled and paradoxical pulls of allegiance. On the one hand, as far as dominant Catholic metropolitan French culture was concerned, Derrida was an outsider several times over, which explains perhaps why he was often to find celebrity abroad before encountering it, so to speak, at home. On the other hand, far from turning aside from the enlightenment imperatives of reason, clarity, and critical debate,

Derrida's response to marginalisation and to his own eccentric place in main-stream French culture was to embrace the European philosophical tradition with renewed passion and commitment, even if – as it invariably did – it meant reminding that tradition of its own past and reading it against the grain of its own received orthodoxy. In order to keep faith with his position as an outsider, Derrida quickly realised, it was necessary precisely to become an insider – not in order to renounce exteriority, but to replace the outside at the centre where it properly-improperly belonged. The challenge was to find a place or, better, a place without a place, simultaneously inside and outside the philosophical tra-dition, *both* as a grateful and respectful guest *and* as a recalcitrant foreign body, not in order to promote consensus, therefore, but to reveal dissensus, and con-scious of the need to exploit all the critical resources bequeathed to him by the philosophical tradition in order that nothing might ever be taken for granted by the philosophical tradition itself. For that tradition was anything but homoge-neous or identical with itself; it was traversed by many unspoken assumptions, discontinuities, internal inconsistencies, tensions, irresolvable paradoxes, slips, silences, absences, and exclusions, all of which it was imperative to address, but the only evidence for which, like some hidden family secret, lay in the family's own historical archive.

The result was an unyielding double stance of fidelity and infidelity. It is in any case impossible to be truly faithful to the legacy of the past, and Derrida was well aware of the paradox. If I scrupulously copy out, in my own hand, adding nothing, subtracting nothing, the opening scenes of *Hamlet*, this may seem to represent a gesture of purest fidelity. But not so, it is infidelity itself, for I do something that neither the author nor the text of *Hamlet* ever did or was or is capable of doing, in which case I find myself betraying both the letter and the spirit of Shakespeare's play.[7] It is however too late for me to do otherwise, and I cannot but accept the inevitability of my betrayal, in which case the only question that remains is how I bear the burden of my betrayal, how I therefore choose or am constrained to invent my relationship with the play, which is what occurs whenever I read it or see it performed.

The paradox is anything but rarefied; it is entirely banal, and has to be confronted anew by every performer who steps on stage, and every reader who picks up the play, and, like the Danish Prince, is enjoined to respond to the words of a father's ghost. To be or not to be, suggests Derrida, citing a fragment from the German poet Friedrich Hölderlin (1770–1843), is first of all to inherit (*SM*, 93–4; 67–8). But all inheritance is necessarily split, and time always out of joint. There is the past, to which it is necessary to pay tribute, if only because without it we cannot say who we are, and because whoever ignores it merely ends up repeating it; and there is the future, unforeseeable, unpredictable, incalculable. And there is no alternative, Derrida argues, but to respond equally to both, even if this means having to confront perpetual, irreconcilable contradiction.

Derrida's own response to the dilemma was a remarkable combination of generosity and vigilance, openness and suspicion. For Derrida, it was absolutely crucial that the two sides of the equation – the past, the future – were not flattened out, synthesised away, and reduced to one. His lifelong commitment, whatever the intellectual consequences, was to this need to respect and affirm difference, division, singularity. It informed all his political, philosophical, and literary thinking. In one of his last interviews, published shortly before his death, Derrida considered for a moment the ambiguous political legacy of the concept of democracy in Europe, whose fate was so often to have been found wanting, but whose promise it was nevertheless essential, Derrida insisted, to continue to affirm. There was no escaping that difficult legacy, its implications for thought, for thinking, and the thinker himself. 'It's true', Derrida agreed, 'you will always find me making this gesture, I have no final justification for it, save that it's who I am, or where I am. I am at war with myself, it's true, you have no idea how much, beyond anything you may guess, and I say contradictory things, which are, shall we say, in real tension with one another, and which make me what I am, are my life's blood, and will be the death of me.' The struggle, he realised, could and would never end. 'Sometimes', he added, 'I see it as a terrifying and painful war, but at the same time I know that's what life is. I will find peace only in eternal rest. So I cannot say I have come to terms with the contradiction, though I also know it is what keeps me alive, and indeed makes me ask the very question you were recalling: "How to learn, how to teach [*Comment apprendre*] how to live?" [cf. *SM*, 13; xvi]' (*AV*, 49).

Life, however, is not something that can either be learned or taught, which is not to say it is not the object of much earnest, anxious, joyful questioning. This was Derrida's point: life is what happens, occurs, takes place, often, as it were, without anyone necessarily being there to take that decision. How, then, here and now, should the relationship between Derrida's life and his work be addressed?

The question admits of no ready answer. The fact is, when books like this choose or are required to deal first with a thinker's life, and then with his or her work, the relationship between the two is not something that may be taken for granted. Is life separate from work? Or is it part of work, and work part of life? For certain critics, life is something that is expressed by the work, while for others it is the work that expresses the life. For others, the work is only valid or valuable because it leads back to life, while for others life itself is strictly irrelevant to the work. These are, in some branches of literary criticism, important debates. But from Derrida's perspective, while life and work are thought as existing in opposition to one another, it matters little how the relationship is construed.

To have some purchase on what is really at stake here, it is necessary, perhaps, to adopt the reverse strategy and begin to consider what it is that joins life and work together. It is soon apparent that what they share is a relationship with death and dying. Dying is the extreme limit of life, its margin, frontier, or border, without which life would not be what it is, but which I cannot know as such since to do so I must pass beyond it and then return. There are manuals on how best to put an end to a life; but there are no instructions on what the experience of dying is like, for it exceeds the possibility of experience, which is why in turn death and killing are events that loom so large in works of fiction. My life is only what it is because I know (or ignore) that, at some point, unknown to me, perhaps tomorrow, the next day or the next, I shall die. Since it always belongs to the future, that dying is something unavailable to me. There is nothing more properly mine, but it is not something I can ever properly claim as such.

At first sight, there could be nothing more different than writing. But what happens when there is writing? What happens is that a trace is left, on paper, on disk, in wax, or on the wet sand, a trace that is no sooner inscribed than it exists without me, and must exist without me, since otherwise it would not be a trace. So this book that you are reading may have been written by a living human (at least I think so); but as soon as these words left my fingers and appeared on my computer screen, they were no longer mine alone. As you read these words, their author may be long dead (how will you tell?), which is also to say, Derrida argues, that the possibility and the inevitability of my dying are already inscribed within these words. Whether I am actually dead or not, as you read these words, then, is less important than the possibility I may be dead, and to that extent am in a sense as good as dead, and dead to these words which (I hope) are still the words I originally intended, but which you are free to interpret as you will.

To understand what is at stake in life, in work, then, it is necessary to consider death: not as grim inevitability, but rather as an unfathomable secret always dividing me from myself. The question is sometimes asked: why live, why write? But there are no answers to such questions. The purpose of life, if one exists, is living; and the purpose of writing, if there is any, is likewise: writing. This of course simplifies nothing. What it does however is to reaffirm the unbounded possibilities of the one and the other, possibilities that, by virtue of the logic of inheritance, are inseparable from a debt owed to the past and to the future. But while there may be ethico-moral or religious precepts which an individual or group may elect to obey, or not, in order to lead a good, decent, or honourable life, there are no rules that teach how to live, or from which it is possible to learn how to live. Life's limits, like those of writing, cannot be decided in advance.

How, then, to carry on? 'I can't go on', answers the narrator in Samuel Beckett's novel *The Unnamable*, and continues, without pause: 'you must go on, I'll go on, you must say words, as long as there are any . . .'[8] When asked by a journalist for the French newspaper *Libération* why he wrote, Beckett replied tersely and to the point, dispensing with both verb and personal pronoun: 'Bon qu'à ça', which meant: 'No good at anything else', 'Only any good at this', 'No good at anything except being or not being B-K-S', in which readers will recognise the outline of a cryptic signature.[9] As the verdict suggests, like Derrida, Beckett was conscious of being a survivor, what French calls a *survivant*, so long as the word is read, as it is by Derrida in the essay 'Living On', in the sense of *both* a living after, in the future, *and* a living boundlessly, in excess of life's limits.

'O day and night, but this is wondrous strange', interjects Horatio. At which Hamlet reminds him: 'There are more things in heaven and earth, Horatio, /Than are dreamt of in your philosophy.' Derrida seems to have agreed. For notwithstanding the formidable critical arsenal deployed by Derrida in his prolonged engagement with Western metaphysics, there was always more to it than that. Most importantly of all, perhaps, though his vigilance was unerring, there was nothing negative about Derrida's thinking, which was carried instead by an irrepressibly affirmative thought of the future: not the future that is a deferred present, calculated, programmed, and determined in advance, and to that extent barely a future at all, but the future which cannot be foreseen, mastered, or regulated, and is still to come (*à-venir*, as the French word *avenir*, future, allows Derrida to say), as threat or promise, without it being possible to say which it is, but without which no literature, no politics, no writing, no otherness, no innovation of any kind would be possible. This other future, for Derrida, one might say, was simply this: another word for life itself.

And so it was, shortly before it was time (time without time) for Derrida's life to end, as it did on 9 October 2004, and just as he had done for many of the friends who had predeceased him, Derrida penned a funeral address, to be read out at his own funeral, written in quotation marks, and in the third person, safe in the knowledge that he would not be there to say it or hear it, but that his words, having already escaped his grasp, had the strength still, or the weakness, to bear witness to the singular mystery of a life. Read aloud by his son Pierre as ritual demanded three days after his death, these, then, were Jacques Derrida's parting words:

'Jacques wanted neither ritual nor oration. He knows from experience what an ordeal it is for the friend who takes on this responsibility. He asks me to thank you for coming and to bless you, he begs you not to be mournful, to think only of the many happy moments which you gave him the chance of sharing with you.

Smile at me, he says, as I will have smiled at you till the end.

Always prefer life and never cease affirming survival [*la survie*: both survival *and* the excess of life].

I love you and am smiling at you from wherever I may be.'    (*RD*, 6–7)

# Chapter 2

# Contexts

## Beginnings

During the early 1950s, as Derrida began to embark on an academic career, the philosophical and literary world in France was still largely dominated by post-war existentialism and, in particular, by the imposing figure of Jean-Paul Sartre, who was still firmly established not only as one of France's leading contemporary philosophers and most prominent campaigning intellectuals, but also as a celebrated novelist, dramatist, and literary critic too. The origins of Sartre's literary and philosophical thinking were many and various. But an important turning point in his intellectual development had been the pre-war encounter in 1933–4 with German phenomenology, most notably with Husserl, whose work, alongside that of Hegel and Heidegger, continued to inform much of Sartre's post-war thinking, though he would often be accused, rightly enough, of interpreting them in idiosyncratic and not always easily defendable ways. Sartre remained however a towering figure, and it was perhaps hardly surprising that, as he sought a path of his own through the complex post-war philosophical landscape, and having encountered Heidegger and Husserl through Sartre, Derrida should first turn his attention, to markedly different effect, to these two key philosophical figures. Derrida however was also determined to strike out on his own. This he did, unfashionably for the time, by concentrating on Husserl's philosophy of science.

Husserl was an original and, in his own terms, revolutionary thinker who, in a series of remarkable publications from 1900 onwards, developed a body of work of redoubtable intricacy, finesse, and complexity. His underlying project, at least in general terms, was relatively simple. Philosophy, from the mid-nineteenth century onwards, he argued, had lost its way, and become confused with a series of drab, disparate, and secondary forms of scientific inquiry incapable of justifying their own conceptual procedures. The task, according to Husserl, was to breathe fresh life into philosophy, reawaken it to its original calling, and provide a new, rigorous, pure foundation for thought. The challenge was to begin again, from the very beginning, and phenomenology, from the Greek *phainomena* (meaning: things as they appear to the senses), was the name Husserl chose for this ambitious new enterprise. He supplied the project with its first goal too, which was to describe in fine, concrete detail how, prior to individual psychology, the world of experience was constituted as meaningful by what he called transcendental consciousness, which was a way of accounting philosophically for the conditions of possibility of experience in general. And in order to reach down to this more fundamental, preliminary level of understanding, he devised an influential methodology, which he termed the phenomenological reduction or *epoché* (from the Greek word meaning suspension of judgement), which involved setting aside, switching off, or putting into parenthesis, as Husserl put it, that 'natural attitude' which included all my prior knowledge or assumptions about the world as it was. 'The phenomenological reduction', commented Emmanuel Levinas, one of Husserl's earliest advocates in France, 'is thus an operation through which the mind suspends the validity of the natural thesis of existence, in order to study its meaning in the thought that has constituted it and that, for its part, is no longer a part of the world but prior to the world. In this returning to primary self-evidence in this manner, I recover at once the origin and the significance of all of my knowledge and the true meaning of my presence in the world.'[1]

This appeal to presence in the world proved deeply attractive. A famous anecdote recounted by Simone de Beauvoir describes how Sartre, in a Paris bar in 1932 or 1933, having been told about Husserl by his friend Raymond Aron, was left speechless with wonder at the notion that phenomenology might turn a seemingly insignificant but concrete object such as an apricot cocktail into a subject of philosophical analysis![2] Sartre's response was to rush out to buy Levinas's pioneering introduction; and as Beauvoir goes on to explain, Husserl's account of the constitutive importance of consciousness gave fresh impetus to Sartre's own staging of the existential project, that movement by which, according to Sartre, far from any static, leaden conception of human nature, my consciousness bursts into the world as an uninhibited creative agent. For if in my consciousness I am essentially free, as Sartre went on to argue in his philosophical work and in such plays as *Les Mouches* (*The Flies*, 1943) or *Les Mains sales* (*Crime Passionel*, 1948), then my inescapable obligation is to affirm that freedom, my own and that of others, in the concrete situation where I find myself. This, then, was the imperative underlying Sartre's commitment to left-wing politics and sustaining the programmatic ethico-moral conception of writing, based on an aesthetics of communication, set out in his influential manifesto of 1948, *Qu'est-ce que la littérature?* (*What is Literature?*).[3]

Sartre's theory of freedom was a powerful, persuasive doctrine that chimed strongly with the preoccupations facing French intellectuals in the wake of the

Occupation. Consensus, however, was not total. This was obvious in the political sphere, where there were often bitter differences regarding the practical political implications of a commitment to the cause of freedom. And there were those, like the critic and novelist Maurice Blanchot and the young Jacques Derrida, who had deep reservations, too, regarding the prescriptive implications of Sartre's theory of literature.[4] Derrida at the time was far from hostile to Sartre's thinking. Though he was uncomfortable with Sartre's attempt to turn literature into a vehicle for ideological and ethico-moral exhortation, he found much to admire in the philosopher's work, as he later explained in a long letter to Claude Lanzmann on the occasion of the fiftieth anniversary of Sartre's founding of the journal *Les Temps modernes* in 1946 (*PM*, 167–213; *N*, 257–92).

There was one reason in particular why Sartre's work continued to interest Derrida. For Sartre's work testified to the enduring importance of a close dialogue between literature and philosophy. Already in the mid-1950s this was one of Derrida's chief intellectual concerns. It was to have been the main focus of the doctoral thesis he never completed, which was essentially concerned, he put it in 1980, with what happened 'between philosophy and literature, science and literature, politics and literature, theology and literature, and psychoanalysis and literature' (*DP*, 443; *TT*, 38). This made it inevitable that in part, and often only implicitly, Derrida would situate his thinking on literature in relation to that of Sartre, which explains why, in the years that followed, Derrida was brought back, time and again, by chance or as a kind of oblique homage to Sartre's prescience, to precisely those authors who had figured importantly in Sartre's early literary essays from the 1940s and 1950s: Maurice Blanchot, Georges Bataille, Francis Ponge, Stéphane Mallarmé, and Jean Genet.

But the manner and extent of Derrida's engagement with Husserl placed him at a distance from ruling existentialist orthodoxy. From his early work on the philosopher, two important traits are worth emphasising. First is that what Derrida found in Husserl was a rigorous commitment to finely detailed philosophical analysis. Like Husserl, Derrida was not a philosopher overly tempted by broad generalities, but persuaded by patient, micrological analysis. From Husserl Derrida also took a certain style of thinking, which might be described as a concern not only with things as they appear in the world, but also, and more radically, with the conditions governing their possibility. Writing on the topic of literature, then, rather than asking what literature in general might be or might mean, Derrida's strategy was to suspend judgement in order to pose the more far-reaching question of the precise conditions of possibility of specific so-called literary texts – even if the answer that came back, as it persistently did, was that any such possibility was never given as such, never pure, and never assured, and that it was in any case no longer possible simply to separate in hierarchical fashion this realm of theoretical possibility from the complex heterogeneity of a given object.

Derrida tells in his 1980 thesis defence how Jean Hyppolite, France's leading Hegel specialist, who had agreed in 1957 to act as Derrida's thesis advisor, confessed to him some ten years later that he had no idea at the time where Derrida's project was heading (*DP*, 442; *TT*, 36–7). Rereading his own early dissertation on Husserl some thirty-six years later in 1990, Derrida was moved rather to express surprise at the remarkable persistence, not to say monotony of his early and subsequent thinking. It was at any event in the engagement with Husserl that the direction of Derrida's work became clear. Husserlian phenomenology, he suggested in 1967, having set out to be a radical revision of traditional metaphysics, had turned out in the end to be another failed attempt at the restoration of metaphysics (*M*, 187–207; 157–73). In the years that followed, Derrida was to explore in ever more detail the dilemma in which this left philosophy: for if it could no longer ground itself in traditional metaphysics, so equally it found itself unable to abandon the legacy that had been bequeathed to it.

Derrida showed in *Speech and Phenomena* that phenomenology ran into particular difficulties in relation to language. Persisting in what was a deeply rooted tradition going back to the Greeks, Husserl had begun by distinguishing and trying to tell apart two types or two aspects of signs: one that expressed the immediacy, presence, and proximity to itself of consciousness, and another marked by secondariness, absence, and distance. But any such separation, Derrida objected, was unsustainable. As far as the sign was concerned, presence was bound to absence, and absence to presence; indeed, both were secondary to a prior movement of deferral and difference, affecting (and thus constituting) both time and space: what Derrida, using a notorious neologism, called *différance* (*M*, 3–29; 3–27).

The reasons for Derrida's coinage, which, as he rightly insisted, was properly neither a word nor a concept, were several (*Po*, 16–20; 8–11). The verb *différer*, in French (deriving from Latin *dis-*, apart, + *ferre*, to carry), has two core meanings. If used transitively, with a direct object, it means: to delay or postpone; if used intransitively, without an object, it means: to differ or be different. In inventing the non-word *différance*, spelled with a letter *a*, contrary to standard usage, Derrida had at least three things in mind. First, it was to emphasise the active dimension of the movement of deferr*ing* or differ*ing*, in much the same way that Levinas, at one stage, in considering how to translate Heidegger, had suggested writing *essance*, instead of *essence*, in order to stress the dynamic character of be-*ing*, which otherwise risked being thought as mere inert fact. Second, since the difference between *différence* and *différance* is not audible in spoken French, Derrida's coinage drew attention to the fact that, in speech itself, something was already at work that exceeded the apparent immediacy, proximity to self, and presence of the voice. Even a language without notation, in other words, was irreducible to an oral or phonetic reality.

There was a third important reason. Since it came from a verb that was both transitive and intransitive, *différance* could be used to indicate a movement that was itself neither active nor passive, but prior to that opposition, just as it preceded, too, numerous other similar binary oppositions: presence and absence, sensible and intelligible, nature and culture, subject and object, and so on. And if *différance* was like a provisional name for what Derrida called the becoming-space of time or the becoming-time of space, and to that extent referred to the movement by which concepts in general might be produced, so it could not itself *already* be a concept (otherwise it would have already presupposed what it sought to explain). It was a provisional name for what had no name, and was therefore not properly identifiable *as such*.

*Différance*, too, crucially for all Derrida's subsequent thinking, did not start or stop with words, but with the trace or tracing, the mark or marking without which not only words, but also much else that was not properly linguistic, would not be possible. *Différance* did not therefore presuppose a theory of language nor indeed any theory of literature (which is not to say it might not have dramatic consequences for both). On the contrary, it was logically prior to the possibility of either and, to that extent, exceeded the boundaries of both. Far from implying a privileging of (human) language, it pointed to a far more general ubiquity of traces and marks (including, among others too numerous to mention, features such as genetic coding, the working of the land, animal tracks, human gesture, memory, experience, socialisation, politics, and so on) all of which implied some kind of mobile, differential articulation, irreducible to presence, but inseparable from life itself in the broadest possible sense.

Heidegger writes somewhere that all great philosophers have but one abiding thought which informs all they say or do. If this is true (and nothing is less certain), then, in Derrida's case, if I may be forgiven this brutal gesture, the thought might be said to be this: that nothing is ever one, but always at least two. For any trace, mark, or inscription to be what it is, there has to be at least two of them. No single beginning or origin is ever available as such. But if repetition is what makes it possible to think sameness or identity, it does so only in so far as it introduces proliferating difference. Repetition and otherness are inseparable. The consequences are far-reaching. Henceforth, instead of guaranteeing it, it seems the very conditions of possibility of identity serve in fact to make it impossible. Identity, in other words, cannot ever be pure, which means it cannot ever properly be identity.

Moreover, between one trace and the next, in so far as there is repetition and difference, there is inevitable and necessary contamination. Everything divides from itself, and no polar or binary opposition can ever be sustained without remainder. What the right hand gives, the left takes away, and vice versa, compromising all presence, positionality, thetic or thematic stability. Prior to presence and absence, prior to being as such, Derrida concludes, there (is) *différance*.

## After structuralism

The argument that no beginning can ever be thought except as an impossibility of beginning was, in a way, nothing new, and necessarily so. But this realisation of the unavailability of the origin as such, implicit in the thought of *différance*, did find a powerful echo in at least one of the key concerns of the next major intellectual movement to gain prominence in France during the 1950s and 1960s: structuralism. Following in phenomenology's footsteps, to which it was profoundly indebted, structuralism was closely associated with advances in anthropology, linguistics, and cultural or literary analysis, and with the names of such leading figures as the anthropologist Claude Lévi-Strauss, the literary critic Roland Barthes, and the psychoanalyst Jacques Lacan. As a movement, structuralism owed its chief inspiration to the work of the Swiss linguist Ferdinand de Saussure, whose *Course in General Linguistics*, based on notes taken by his students at the University of Geneva, was first published posthumously in 1916. It amounted mainly to an attempt to apply linguistic theory to a broad range of extra-linguistic or language-based socio-cultural phenomena, from kinship rules to face painting, from indigenous myths to advertising, movies, and literary texts.

What made this huge expansion possible was a fresh understanding of the workings of human language. During much of the nineteenth century, the study of language had been dominated by questions of origins: how and where language in general had begun, how actual languages had developed, and where particular words or expressions had first appeared. This had given rise to much important and influential work. The quest for the origin of language proved, however, fruitless. But in the early years of the new century an important shift took place as Saussure began to argue that language was not a nomenclature, i.e. a list of names related first and foremost to the objects to which they referred, or to other words used to refer to that same object, but functioned instead as a system or structure.

What counted now was not the hypothetical origin of language, nor even the history of isolated words, but relationships between elements in a structure: on the one hand, the arbitrary (or, more accurately, unmotivated) relationship, grounded not in nature but in convention, between an acoustic image or graphic representation (what Saussure famously called the signifier) and the conceptual content of the sign (the signified), and, on the other, the relationships between signs, which were primarily, Saussure argued, relationships of difference. 'In language', he famously wrote, 'there are only differences *without positive terms*.'[5] In other words, to understand the meaning or value of a given term in a language, it was necessary to situate it within the network of differential relationships that defined it. Language, Saussure suggested, was in this regard much like the game of chess. What material was used to make the pieces, how they were made, or even how they looked, all this was of no importance, so long as the pieces could be differentiated from one another according to agreed rules. In turn, the significance or function of each piece depended purely on the state of play in the game as summed up by all the possible legitimate or legal moves existing at any one point.[6]

Saussure's influence extended far beyond linguistics proper. It prompted a renewed interest in the norms and conventions governing socio-cultural activity in general, and it was not long before literature too was being examined from a similar perspective. One crucial figure in the history of this encounter between the science of language and literary criticism was the linguist and poetician Roman Jakobson, whose career took him, during the first half of the twentieth century, from his native Moscow to Prague, and then via Scandinavia to New York, and finally to Harvard. At each step of the way, Jakobson, a keen student of both Husserl and Saussure, exerted a defining influence over a host of different movements and schools of thought which, added together, read like a manual of modern literary theory: Russian Formalism, Prague School linguistics, American New Criticism, and French structuralist poetics, not forgetting Lévi-Straussian anthropology and Lacanian psychoanalysis.

'The subject of literary scholarship', Jakobson wrote in 1921, 'is not literature in its totality, but literariness (*literaturnost*'), i.e. that which makes of a given work a work of literature.'[7] With these words, modern literary theory may be said to have been born. For what the concept of *literaturnost'* sought to identify was no longer what a particular literary text might mean, what ideas or emotions its author might have wanted to express, or how the work might reflect its social or cultural environment, but what constituted it *as* literature. Art was device, argued the leading Russian Formalist theorist Victor Shklovsky four years later; it was, he explained, 'a way of experiencing the artfulness of an object; the object is not important'.[8] Literature, then, was a 'making strange' of habitual perceptions, achieved through the linguistic or aesthetic self-consciousness characterising all poetic language in general – what Jakobson would later describe as the stress laid on the message for its own sake – and which found its most splendid embodiment in Lawrence Sterne's eighteenth-century masterpiece *Tristram Shandy*, of which Shklovsky famously wrote in 1921 that it was 'the most typical novel in world literature'.[9]

In the early decades of the twentieth century, the path trodden by the Formalists and their followers, which ideologues of both right and left did their utmost to destroy, was often lonely and beleaguered. But by the 1960s it had become a thoroughfare. Myth analysis, narrative grammar, plot analysis, poetics, structural analysis, narratology, textual semiotics: these are just some of the names of the diverse theoretical approaches to literary and other texts that were devised in the years that followed the Formalists' initial breakthrough, and which are now an essential part in the literary studies syllabus in general. But despite their many disagreements on matters of detail, what these different versions of literary theory all have in common is the legacy of *literaturnost'* itself, the assumption that there is a distinctive, autonomous entity called poetic or literary language, of which it is possible to ask what it *is*, and that this entity can be described and analysed on the basis of the Saussurean concept of the sign, that is, as a series of rule-governed utterances shaped by convention, and reducible to the combination of an acoustic or graphic representation and a conceptual or thematic content, otherwise known as a signifier and a signified.

By the mid-1960s, faced with this growing proliferation of language-based methodologies, it had become increasingly urgent, as far as Derrida was concerned, to subject this new theoretical consensus to critical scrutiny. His intervention marked a turning point: the publication of *De la grammatologie* in 1967. In the book, Derrida began by re-examining two of the most important bodies of work that had helped found contemporary structuralism: the early twentieth-century linguistics of Saussure and the post-war structural anthropology of Lévi-Strauss, which Derrida traced back to an earlier, exemplary figure, to whom both Saussure and Lévi-Strauss acknowledged an intellectual debt: the eighteenth-century philosopher, novelist, and autobiographer Jean-Jacques Rousseau. At work in the thought of all three, Derrida discovered, was a questionable opposition, reminiscent of what he had already found in Husserl, between a trustworthy, self-present form of language identified with speech, and its treacherous, parasitic double, called writing.

This separation of language into two hierarchically contrasted, antagonistic states, and the privileging of speech over writing had deep roots, reaching back to the Greeks, and had found exemplary expression in the dialogues of Plato, who, in this regard, as in so many others, stood at the outset as the founding father of metaphysics. But Rousseau too had maintained the same privilege of speech over writing and in an unfinished, hitherto little-read essay dealing with the question of the origin of languages (all the more revealing because of that neglect) had denounced writing as something essentially artificial, unnatural, and corrupting, what he elsewhere termed a 'dangerous supplement'. Saussure too, in thinking of the sign as the joining together of a signified and a signifier, even as he had broken with tradition by insisting on the inseparability of the two, similarly found himself reactivating, no doubt unwittingly, the age-old philosophical opposition between the intelligible and sensible, mind and body, content and form, which relied in the end on the priority of signified over signifier, and the immediacy of speech over the disobedient trickery of writing, the model for which was that of God speaking to Moses (*Po*, 28–34; 18–23). 'The age of the sign', Derrida remarked, 'is essentially theological' (*G*, 25; 14).

Derrida's strategy, however, was not to claim a better, superior vantage point from which he might show Plato, Rousseau, Saussure, or Lévi-Strauss the error of their ways. It was to emphasise that, already in each of their actual texts, there was implicit, covert, reluctant recognition of the fact that the privilege conferred on speech was logically unsustainable. In a word, the means to unpick the metaphysical tradition were already secretly at work in that tradition itself. The logic of the supplement was a case in point. As Derrida pointed out, to devastating effect, the term implied two contrary but inseparable things. A supplement was not only an indication of abundance, a kind of additional resource adding itself to an existing plenitude; it was proof that there was already something deficient in what it was required to supplement – in much the same way that a substitute at football, for instance, may serve equally as a sign of the strength in depth available to the winning team, or as a symptom of the losing team's inability to score at all (*G*, 208; 145). So, if speech needed a supplement, it was not simply a token of its boundless presence; it was because it was not as fully present to itself as it believed.

Indeed, Derrida observed, however much philosophers since Plato had viewed writing with suspicion, this did not prevent all the negative traits that were displaced onto writing – unreliability, duplicity, loss, absence, death – from being necessarily already at work in speech *and* writing alike. This was why Derrida proposed a radical rethinking of the relationship between the two. It was essential, of course, not simply to reverse the hierarchy, and begin to privilege writing over speech, body over mind, or signifier over signified, for instance, which would be merely perverse. The whole configuration needed to be recast. To do so, Derrida began to articulate a third term, irreducible to speech or writing in the conventional, received, metaphysical sense, which he called '*archi-écriture*', 'arche-writing' (from the Greek *arché*, beginning), or, more simply 'writing'. In much the same way that *différance* is not part of a theory of language as such, so too arche-writing is not a property of language, which it logically preceded. 'The fact is', Derrida explained, 'arche-writing, as the movement of différance and an irreducible arche-synthesis, which at one and the same time, and as a single possibility, opens temporalisation, the relation to the other, and language, cannot, in so far as it is the condition of any language system, form part of that language system itself and be positioned as an object within its field' (*G*, 88; 60; translation modified).

In proposing the term 'arche-writing', which he more often than not replaced by the word 'writing', Derrida was taking a calculated risk. The problem was, he argued, there was no place of thought outside the Western philosophical tradition to which it might be possible to appeal or to retreat. In any case, within that tradition there were immense resources which it was foolish to ignore. This was why Derrida chose an already existing, arguably compromised word, 'writing', to say something radically new. And what this emphasised in turn was that writing, in this new radical sense, rather than standing outside philosophy, named something already secretly at work within it, but which had to be prised away from the conventional meanings ascribed to it.

In maintaining the term 'writing', but giving to it an entirely different place and function in his own writing, Derrida's chief concern was to intervene in contemporary debates, which increasingly turned on the supposedly pre-eminent role played by language in the Saussurean sense. But there was a danger, which was hard, perhaps impossible to avoid. It was that hasty or careless readers might leap to the conclusion that it was enough to invert the received hierarchy of speech over writing. And this, as *Of Grammatology* became more widely read, was something commentators rarely failed to do, which contributed to no small extent to the controversy surrounding Derrida's work, and explains why he was so often presented by his detractors, particularly in the English-speaking world, as perversely bent on turning so-called common sense on its head.

The implications of Derrida's analysis of phonocentrism, as the unchallenged privilege of speech over writing was now termed, were many, and Derrida was to spend much of the next thirty-seven years exploring and exploiting them in a series of ever-changing contexts and settings. In the process, Derrida's thinking acquired a label or slogan: deconstruction. Admittedly, the word, initially written with a hyphen in the original French, was first used by Derrida himself, in the first essay of his to appear in English, 'Structure, Sign, and Play in the Discourse of the Human Science', where the term was explicitly linked to the question of inheritance (*WD*, 414; 357). He also used it again in *Of Grammatology*, writing, for instance, that the '"rationality" . . . commanding the enlarged and radicalised concept of writing no longer derives from any logos [*logos*, from the Greek: reason, rationality, discourse, logic], and inaugurates the destruction, not the demolition, but the de-sedimentation and de-construction of all meanings that have their source in the meaning of logos' (*G*, 21; 10; translation slightly modified). But though he explained at length his reasons for using the word in a letter to his Japanese friend Toshihiko Izutsu in July 1983 (*Psy*, 387–93; *BB*, 270–6), and became resigned to it in the end, if only because of the currency it had achieved, Derrida was reluctant to endorse the term, since it equated his work with the unthinking application of a standard and standardised methodology, a notion deeply at odds with the intervention he had wanted to make in suggesting the word de-construction in the first place.

There were further important consequences stemming from Derrida's expanded and revised concept of writing which were also relevant for the style and manner of his own work. For the philosophical tradition had not only privileged speech over writing, it had also preferred particular canonic languages over others. Hegel in the *Science of Logic* famously complimented German idiom for its use of the same verb, *aufheben*, to mean to retain *and* to abolish, and thus make a decisive contribution to speculative thinking not available to whoever had only Latin.[10] More than a century later, in 1946, in a famous letter to Jean Beaufret rebutting what he saw as Sartre's serious misreading of his work, Heidegger made a similar point, claiming philosophy could properly only take place in Greek or, failing that, in German. As for the French, he told an interviewer in 1966, '[w]henever they begin thinking, they speak in German; they assure me, they simply cannot manage in their own language'.[11] The gesture may seem odd, but other philosophers at other times have made similar moves, regarding for instance mathematics or ordinary language as privileged vehicles for philosophical inquiry.

For Derrida, however, all such attempts to rank one language or idiom over another were deeply questionable. The logic of *différance* meant that language and languages were by definition multiple, and there was no justification, other than authoritarian dogma, for setting one idiom aside as being more adequate or truthful than others. Derrida went so far as to suggest that if he were to venture ('God forbid', he added) a single definition of deconstruction, this would be it: a responsiveness to language transfer and transference, to the fact that there was, as he put it in French, *plus d'une langue*, meaning both *more* than one language and no more *one* language (*MM*, 38; 15). The singularity of idiom was inescapable, and could not be effaced, only ever affirmed. And it became an increasingly characteristic signature feature of Derrida's own writing, in particular from the early to mid-1970s onwards, as he left behind some of the rhetorical norms of orthodox philosophical discourse, that he should exploit with virtuosity – to the despair of his translators – the many resources of French idiom and other languages, too. Derrida's purpose was not playful indulgence for its own sake, as commentators sometimes mistakenly assume. For in exploring the complexities of idiom, Derrida was making an important philosophical point: that there was a density, materiality, and labyrinthine weave to thinking, and that, like writing, thinking was an unpredictable and sometimes startling event which it was essential to countersign as such – as he did, for instance, after discovering in the letters, papers, and drawings of the writer Antonin Artaud the strange word *subjectile* (which is better established in English than it is in French, and refers to the material or bodily surface upon which a painting is made or a text inscribed), which gave rise to a lengthy and remarkable homage to Artaud, which was also a kind of signature piece on Derrida's part, entitled 'Forcener le subjectile' ('To Unsense the Subjectile').[12]

## Signature event context

*Of Grammatology* is an imposing monument, and the place where most conscientious readers of Derrida might want to start. It is, however, a demanding text, particularly for readers less familiar with philosophical tradition than Derrida's more immediate audience. In the remaining part of this chapter, then, in an inevitably partial and schematic way, I want to review some of the key emphases in Derrida's argument not by concentrating on *Of Grammatology*, but by turning instead to a shorter, more accessible text: 'Signature événement contexte' ('Signature Event Context') (*M*, 367–93; 309–30). This was first delivered at a conference in Montreal on the theme of communication in 1971; when it subsequently appeared in English in 1977, it prompted an immediate critical riposte from the American philosopher and linguistician, John R. Searle, to whom Derrida replied at some length later that year, though the controversy contrived to smoulder on for a decade more, as the volume *Limited Inc*, which brings most of these texts together, amply testifies.

Derrida's paper is in four parts, and comprises a preamble and three main sections devoted in reverse order to each of the three terms given in the title. Like all good conference delegates, Derrida announces the purpose of his intervention early on: it is to demonstrate 'why a context is never absolutely determinable or, better, in what way its determination is never assured or saturated' (*M*, 369; 310). From this central proposition, Derrida adds, flow two important corollaries, namely that the standard, received concept of (linguistic or non-linguistic) context, among others, is theoretically inadequate; and that it is necessary (as Derrida proposes in *Of Grammatology*) to effect *both* a generalisation *and* a displacement of the concept of writing (*M*, 369; 310–11).

Derrida begins with a question, of particular relevance at a conference on the topic of communication, which is this: 'Is it certain [*assuré*: assured, guaranteed] that to the word *communication* there corresponds a single, univocal, rigorously graspable, transmissible, i.e., communicable concept?' (*M*, 367; 309; translation modified). In other words, does the term communication communicate, as it should, a clearly communicable content? Plainly, the word *communication* has a number of divergent senses, particularly in French, where it can mean the transfer or transmission of linguistic meaning (as it tends to do in English), but where it can also refer to the imparting of (non-linguistic) force or movement, and where it is also the word used for a paper given at a conference.

This initial overview allows Derrida to make several points. First, usage shows that the verb *communiquer*, to communicate, does not always mean a transfer of sense: this meaning is only one among several. It would, however, be theoretically incoherent to organise these different possible senses of the word according to a hierarchy that would start with the so-called literal meaning, and move on to so-called figurative or metaphorical meanings, which is what dictionaries generally do, since this would be to presuppose the very thing, i.e. the transfer of meaning, that the inquiry into the meaning(s) of the word *communiquer* hoped to clarify. What this indicates in turn, as opening the pages of any dictionary will demonstrate, is that there is no place outside of words to communicate what those words actually mean, since meaning can only be communicated through the use of other words. The result is a perpetual circle, without proper beginning or proper ending, and a speaker or writer, in order to begin, has to presume, at least provisionally, as does Derrida at the outset of his paper, that within a given context there exists a minimal degree of consensus about the meaning(s) of certain words, as in this case the meaning of the word 'communication' as used within the context of a philosophical congress on the topic of communication.

As readers of literature know, in determining meaning and removing possible ambiguities, context is crucial. But what is a context? Is context part of text or text part of context? Where does context begin or end? How are its boundaries determined, and who is to say what it includes or excludes? These are far-reaching questions. But there is nothing abstract about them. They are precisely what is at stake each time a critic or student starts interpreting a text or writing an essay.

I have lingered on Derrida's preamble for two reasons. First, Derrida begins by dramatising the very question he is addressing. What his beginning shows, in other words – and this is what Derrida will go on to articulate in the body of the paper itself – is that it is impossible properly to begin. The only possible beginning is an impossibility of properly beginning. What Derrida says is repeated, mirrored, and confirmed in the way in which he says it. This is a common rhetorical strategy on Derrida's part. Almost invariably, by a logic that is as remorseless as it is strategic, readers will find that the opening words by Derrida serve to instantiate or exemplify the questions addressed in more explicitly philosophical or theoretical terms in the text itself. It would be a mistake, however, to see this as mere playfulness on Derrida's part; it is a measure of his acute sense of the singularity of context(s), and an indication of his responsibility towards his audience(s), and of his desire, precisely, to communicate.

This brings me to my second point about Derrida's preamble. The question it asks is a fundamental one. Where to begin? Where to begin thinking, writing, reading? More particularly, perhaps, where to begin reading Derrida? Indirectly, Derrida's beginning supplies an answer to these questions. For if it is impossible properly to begin, there can be no pure, authorised, authoritative beginning. There is no alternative, in other words, than to begin in precisely that specific, singular context in which, by chance or design, one is situated. This in turn means, first, that there is an inescapable violence, a necessary abruptness, associated with all attempts at beginning; and, second, that all speaking or writing is situated, here and now, in a given context, even if it is an essential and irreducible aspect of that context that it cannot ever be determined absolutely. And there is a third implication too, which is a political one, Derrida insists, which is that deconstruction, if such a thing exists, cannot *not* confront the question of the place where it finds itself. More often than not, though not always, far from it, that place is an academic institution, which was one of the reasons for Derrida's long-standing interest in institutions in general and in the institution of the university in particular.[13] This was also why, in part,

Derrida in 1977 insisted that deconstruction 'is not a discursive or theoretical matter, but a practico-political one, and one that always occurs in what are called, in rather hasty and summary fashion, institutional structures' (*PC*, 536; 508; translation modified).

The second part (or first part proper, or, perhaps better, first part improper) of Derrida's paper now follows. It is entitled 'Writing and Telecommunication' and takes the reader on a detour through the history of philosophy. For the concept of communication brings with it a legacy which it is essential to reconsider, since to ignore it would be to risk naively reproducing it. There is common agreement, it seems, says Derrida, that one major form of communication is writing, and that writing is seen as having the power to extend the horizon of possible communication across both time and space. But though its range may vary, the space of communication, as far as this standard view is concerned, Derrida argues, remains essentially homogeneous (*M*, 369–70; 311). Over the next few pages, Derrida goes on to explore by way of example the ideas of the eighteenth-century French philosopher Etienne Condillac, whose work is particularly relevant in that it explicitly addresses the relationship between communication and writing, with the latter being construed as an external accessory or supplement, the purpose of which is to compensate for the unavailability or absence of the person I wish to address (*M*, 372–4; 313–15). But absence in Condillac, Derrida argues, is determined in partial or derived manner, i.e. solely as the absence of the addressee, and only as a gradual diminution of presence (which always come first). Condillac does not consider the possible absence of the sender of the message (think of a message in a bottle, or even this book you are reading), nor does he take account of the possibility that the message may – and must – continue to be legible even if it is impossible fully to retrieve what its author may have intended: think of that obscure one-line fragment, found in Nietzsche's posthumous papers, claiming: 'I have forgotten my umbrella', which, opening only to close again, or closing only to open again, like all umbrellas, no doubt signifies something, suggests Derrida – but what? (*E*, 103–23; 122–42).

Traditionally, what distinguishes writing from speech is the role played by absence. But what kind of absence is really at stake? An absence, replies Derrida, that, rather than being treated as a diminution of presence, i.e. a presence retained, postponed, deferred, the better for it to be retrieved later, needs to be thought of instead as a radical interruption of presence: as a kind of always impending but inescapable death. For what makes writing possible at all, irrespective of the presence or absence of any given addressee, is the repeatability, or iterability of the writing, as Derrida calls it, bringing together under one head, by way of the term *itara*, the idea that what repetition always brings, though it may look like identity, is always something different, singular, and other. He explains:

> My 'written communication', in other words, has to remain legible [*lisible*, readable] in spite of the absolute disappearance [*disparition*: the word is often used to mean death] of every determined addressee in general for it to function as writing, that is, for it to be readable. It must be repeatable – iterable – in the absolute absence of the addressee or the empirically determinable entirety of addressees. This iterability (*iter*, meaning: *once again*, is said to come from Sanskrit *itara*, meaning: *other*, and everything that follows may be read as the exploitation of the logic binding repetition to alterity) structures the mark of writing itself, and indeed does so whatever kind of writing it is (whether pictographic, hieroglyphic, ideographic, phonetic, or alphabetic, to use these outdated categories).    (*M*, 375; 315; translation modified)

What counts, then, is this iterability of the sign; and what holds for the absence of the addressee will also apply to the absence of the addressor (*M*, 376; 316). As you read these words, I am necessarily absent, possibly dead. But this does not prevent you from reading them. Even if I were still alive, it would make no difference. My words have no need of me to carry on making themselves readable and, in the process, signifying many things that, believe me, I never intended, and which never once occurred to me when I wrote them. Which was why Socrates, in Plato's *Phaedrus*, it may be remembered, famously judged writing to be so unreliable. 'Once a thing is put in writing', he argues, 'the composition, whatever it may be, drifts all over the place, getting into the hands not only of those who understand it, but equally of those who have no business with it; it doesn't know how to address the right people, and not address the wrong. And when it is ill-treated and unfairly abused it always needs its parent to come to its help, being unable to defend or help itself.'[14]

Although the classic view of writing does not thematise iterability as such, it does go some way towards registering its implications, if only in so far as it associates writing with absence. Indeed, the traditional concept of writing, Derrida continues, can be characterised by three main assumptions: first, that a written sign is a mark that lasts, or remains, and is not reducible to any given present moment; second, that it can always be detached from its original context, and grafted on to another; and third, that the sign is always at a distance from the present thing to which it refers, which is why it can be cited, or used again to refer to another thing.

But what would happen, asks Derrida, if each of these traits, rather than being seen to affect *only* writing, were found instead to be common to *both* speech *and* writing? This is what Derrida now goes on to show. Iterability, in other words, he argues, is not a feature of written language alone, but of *all* language, *both* spoken *and* written in general. For if all signs are by definition repeatable, there are no limits to that movement of repetition. Any sign, in so far as it repeated, can be detached from its context; and if it is true of all signs, it must be true of spoken as well as written ones (as any audio recording will immediately confirm). Derrida writes:

> This structural possibility of being weaned [*sevrée*, separated, taken off the breast] from its referent or its signified (and therefore from communication and its context) seems to me to make of every mark, even an oral one, a grapheme in general, that is, . . . the non-present *remainder* [*restance*, a remaining] of a differential mark cut off [*coupée*, severed] from its supposed 'production' or origin.
>
> (*M*, 378; 318; translation modified)

Logically, then, if *all* forms of language, spoken *and* written, depend on iterability, it follows that the conventional distinction between speech and writing no longer holds. It might even appear that, rather than writing being a degraded form of speech, it is speech itself that is more like a sub-set of writing as traditionally conceived. So there may be grounds (a) for reversing or inverting the received hierarchy between speech and writing. But in itself this would hardly be enough. It would not alter the essential structure or paradigm within which thought is operating. It is therefore necessary (b) to displace the conventional concept of writing, and reconfigure it in such a way that it might account for *both* speech *and* writing *in their conventional senses*. What is crucial here is to note these two distinct, albeit inseparable stages in Derrida's argument, for if the word deconstruction means anything at all, it should be understood as denoting the necessity of *both* these operations (*Po*, 56–7; 41–2): an inversion, by which a hierarchy is reversed (with speech, for instance, being seen to rely on traits, such as absence or repetition, that hitherto have been solely attributed to writing); *and* a displacement, by which the conventional concept of writing, though provisionally now dominant, is shifted, dismantled, and reinvented as something radically other.

At this stage in Derrida's paper, there now follows a discussion of Husserl, the purpose of which is to develop further the implications of iterability as the condition of possibility of language, written and spoken, at the end of which he returns to the question of context with which he began, in order to set out more explicitly what was at stake in his opening remarks. And Derrida notes as follows:

> Every sign, linguistic or non-linguistic, spoken or written (in the usual sense of this opposition), as a small or large unity, can be *cited*, put in quotation marks; thereby it can break with every given context, and engender infinitely new contexts in an absolutely non-saturable fashion. This does not suppose that the mark is valid outside its context but on the contrary that there are only contexts without any absolute centre of anchorage. This citationality, this duplication or duplicity, this iterability of the mark is not an accident or an anomaly, but is that (beyond normal and abnormal) without which a mark could not even have a so-called 'normal' functioning. What would be a mark that could not be cited? And whose origin might not get lost in the process?
>
> (*M*, 381; 320–1; translation modified)

Derrida now moves to the next section, on the topic of 'Parasites', focussing on the work of the Oxford language philosopher J. L. Austin. He begins by situating his positive interest in Austin, which is four-fold. For in *How to Do Things With Words*, Austin famously identifies a set of utterances he proposes to call performatives, which, instead of describing, stating, or reporting a given set of affairs, carry out, or perform what they say they are doing even as they do it, like the expression 'I do', for instance, when uttered in the course of the marriage ceremony, says Austin, or such phrases as 'I name this ship the *Queen Elizabeth*', as uttered when smashing the bottle against the stern, or 'I give and bequeath my watch to my brother', as occurring in a will.[15] Importantly, for Derrida, Austin breaks with tradition by no longer considering acts of language solely as acts of communication; by thinking communication as the communication of (verbal or illocutionary) force, rather than of constituted meanings; by identifying a type of language that has its referent in itself and not outside it; and, perhaps most importantly of all, by exploring a form of language that is no longer bound by the opposition between what is claimed to be true or false (*M*, 382–3; 321–2). There is much, therefore, that Derrida finds original and innovative in Austin's work. He goes on to argue, however, that Austin encounters serious difficulties in his account precisely because of the metaphysical assumptions he has inherited without adequately questioning them.

Much hinges, as before, on the concept of context. Performatives, as Austin points out, are massively dependent on contextual conventions. 'Speaking generally', he argues, 'it is always necessary that the *circumstances* in which the words are uttered should be in some way, or ways, *appropriate*.'[16] In order to baptise a child successfully, I must be authorised, for instance, by a church, and have to observe various other legal and cultural norms. But it is always possible for those rules to be ignored, perverted, or fall victim to interference. I may be pretending, or acting, or poking fun, or simply quoting for the purposes of this discussion. Performatives, then, sometimes do not work, as Austin freely acknowledges from the outset. There are conditions that must be respected: 'I must not be joking, for example', he says, 'nor writing a poem',[17] and Austin goes on to discuss at some length the difference between happy and unhappy, felicitous and infelicitous acts of language. His methodological assumption, however, is that such parasitic practices, as he calls them, which include using performatives on stage or in a poem, may, for the purpose of analysis, be disregarded. 'I mean, for example, the following', Austin declares: 'a performative utterance will, for example, be *in a peculiar way* hollow or void if said by an actor on the stage, or if introduced in a poem, or spoken in soliloquy. [. . .] Language in such circumstances is in special ways – intelligibly – used not seriously, but in ways *parasitic* upon its normal use – ways which fall under the doctrine of the *etiolations* of language. All this we are *excluding* from consideration.'[18]

Derrida, however, objects. Austin's methodological assumption, he argues, involves far more than methodology. It amounts to a problematic and unjustifiable limitation of the object of inquiry itself, which cannot *not* compromise and invalidate the inquiry. For Derrida insists that the failure of performatives cannot be set aside like some unfortunate accident. It has to be explained by the structure of performatives in general. This is a common strategy on Derrida's part. He argues consistently throughout that, if the business of philosophy or theory is to specify the conditions of possibility of an event, for those conditions to be truly what they claim to be, they must be able to account for both the success *and* failure of the event. So the failure of performatives cannot be written off; it must be seen as a consequence of the structure of all performatives, in which case it becomes necessary to rethink the logic commanding so-called successful performatives, in so far as they are necessarily always marked by the possibility of failure, and by the ghostly, virtual prospect of that outcome. For if the possibility of failure exists, as it does, then no performative, even an allegedly successful one, can be deemed *wholly* to have succeeded. Failure, too, is only ever partial. Felicity and infelicity cannot be opposed. The one always already inhabits the other. The outside is already inside.

This, then, is the paradox: what is expelled as incompatible with the pure enactment of performatives turns out in fact to be the very condition of possibility of performatives occurring at all. Derrida explains:

> The question is therefore this: is this general possibility [of what Austin describes as parasitic] necessarily that of a failure or trap into which language can *fall* or be lost as though into an abyss outside it or facing it? What is the status of interference [*parasitage*]? In other words, does the generality of the risk admitted by Austin *surround* language like a kind of outer ditch, a place of external perdition into which speech might be unable to go, which it might avoid by staying home, in itself, sheltered by its essence or *telos*? Or indeed is the risk, on the contrary, its internal and positive condition of possibility? this outside its inside? the very force and law of its emergence?     (*M*, 387; 325; translation modified)

In the last section of his paper, Derrida goes on to consider signatures. Here too standard logic receives another startling reversal and displacement. A signature is an essential act of language, without which many things, from credit cards to works of literature, including speech acts themselves, would barely occur at all. Their purpose, it seems, is to guarantee authenticity. Signatures only prove authenticity, however, because they are repeatable, i.e., because the signature I put at the bottom of the traveller's cheque *more or less* exactly replicates my signature at the top. But precisely for that very reason, because there is necessary repetition, the threat of inauthenticity, duplication, or forgery, can never be excluded. Indeed, what iterability shows is that an authentic signature shares the same conditions of possibility as an inauthentic one, and it is impossible to have the one without the threat or promise of the other. All fall subject to the necessary possibility of unauthorised duplication, impropriety, and interference: what Derrida later, using a portmanteau coinage, calls *destinerrance* (i.e. destination + errancy) (*AT*, 86; 162). And it is not just that any signature is a speech act, it is that every speech act is itself a signature, which, by the logic of iterability, can never in fact, wholly, purely, or without loss, lay claim to what it declares or writes in its own name. So although all speech acts may be signatures, this does not mean that any signature is an exemplary speech act; for what iterability implies is that there are no pure, exemplary forms of anything. The only law, Derrida argues, is the law of impurity and heterogeneity.

It is essential to realise at this stage that the implications of Derrida's analysis are far from negative. They are irreducibly affirmative. The necessary provision that no context is ever saturable, but always contains an excess or remainder, a gap where another, perhaps you or I, is allowed, invited, even required to intervene – this is the reason I can read Derrida and quote his work, and the reason others, in turn, can read and quote from Shakespeare, Dickens, Proust, or Woolf, for, in doing these things, each of us creates a new context, which itself is never saturable, and which it will fall to others to supplement in their turn.

And the necessary provision that any mark can always be a re-mark, i.e. can be marked for a second time, remarked upon, brought to attention not only as a meaning but as a word, cited and put at a distance, or attributed to another, and its meaning qualified or modified – this in turn is the very reason literature is possible. For just as the eighteenth-century English novel began by taking the fallen epics of yesteryear or the letters of young women or the diaries and memoirs of travellers, and transformed them into works of fiction, so elsewhere too, history shows, literature began by displacing words from one context to another: without end.

Contexts are crucial, but cannot be exhaustively described. The contexts described here, then, are far from exhausting the many possibilities inseparable from Derrida's work. They are necessarily incomplete; and there will always be many further contexts to be considered, some (but only some) of which will be the subject of the next chapter.

# Chapter 3

# Work

## A double session

*I*

Early in 1969, some eighteen months or so after the appearance of *L'Ecriture et la différence* (*Writing and Difference*) and *De la grammatologie* (*Of Grammatology*), Derrida was invited to give a paper at a meeting of the Groupe d'études théoriques (or Theoretical Study Group) recently set up by the Paris avant-garde literary journal *Tel Quel.*[1] This was an important occasion; and it gave Derrida the opportunity of presenting what remains his most fully developed account of the relationship between philosophy and literature and of that famous leading question: 'What is literature?'

Before Derrida began speaking, each audience member was handed a single sheet of paper, on which there stood two quotations, in differing typefaces. The first, much the longer of the two, was an extract from Plato's *Philebus*, running across the upper third of the handout, and continuing down the left-hand side, while the second, slotted into the lower right-hand corner, consisted of a brief, relatively little-known prose text by the late nineteenth-century French poet Stéphane Mallarmé (1842–98) (*D*, 201; 175). A number of additional quotations from the poet's work were chalked up in white on the blackboard, supplementing Derrida's handout, which was typed up in black on white. An old-fashioned chandelier illuminated proceedings. Derrida's talk was untitled, for reasons he went on to explain; a second session, also untitled, had been scheduled for the following week.

There were many reasons for this elaborate staging. The first had to do with what I have already described as the impossibility of properly beginning, with its two corollaries, i.e. that every discourse is inscribed within a context, but that it is impossible fully to contain that context, if only because any one text always led to another, and another. Even as Derrida sat down to speak, then, his own words were part of a context framed, though hardly exhausted, by the names Plato and Mallarmé, even to the point of already including the phrase:

'the speaker takes his seat' (*D*, 207; 181), which Derrida duly quoted and acted out, and which had featured almost exactly seventy-nine years earlier to the day in Mallarmé's own tribute to the memory of his late friend, the poet Villiers de l'Isle-Adam. There were other concerted efforts at repetition (or iteration) on Derrida's part. For when Mallarmé died, some eight years after Villiers, he left behind a series of drafts or notes (the majority of which, following the poet's instructions, were burnt shortly after his death) belonging to an unfinished work known to literary history only as *Le Livre* (*The Book*) – part poem, part liturgical ritual, part theatrical performance – one of the provisions of which, in at least one of its versions, was that, like Derrida's own paper, it should take place over two sessions. One of the quotations on Derrida's blackboard confirmed as much by explicitly evoking this 'double session' (*D*, 202; 176); and it was no surprise, by a mixture of happenstance and calculation, that the expression 'The Double Session', like a single sheet of paper folded into two, should also become the title of Derrida's untitled paper, to which it therefore referred at least twice over, before then serving once again, not for the first time, as the title of what you are reading.

But for the moment the two sessions remained nameless. This too was a gesture of acknowledgement towards Mallarmé, since the poet had himself voiced deep reservations about the power of titles to dominate or usurp the texts they headed. But, like Derrida, Mallarmé was also aware that it was impossible *not* to have a title (and if a writer refuses to supply one, what invariably happens, as countless untitled poems testify, is that the opening words of a text become its title). But though titles can become so dominant as to pre-empt the way a text is read (think for instance of the title of Joyce's *Ulysses*), they can also have the opposite effect by hanging over the text, postponing and complicating its meaning (think again of the title of Joyce's *Ulysses*). Any title is therefore at least double: it announces what a text may mean, but introduces an unavoidable, not always unwelcome degree of suspense. It refers to what will come, while also deferring it; and at this point Derrida might well have gestured, by way of example, towards the old-fashioned chandelier in the room where he was speaking: a dominant presence, certainly, but one that cast both light *and* shadow over everything below.

This double status of the title, simultaneously framing and prolonging the text, gave Derrida his opening. First, there was the question of what made it possible for a phrase like 'the double session' not only to migrate from one time or place to another, from 1890 to 1969 (and 2007), from Mallarmé to Derrida and beyond, but also, as it did so, alongside its many other possible meanings, to retain the uncanny ability to point silently to itself, so that the words 'the double session' might be taken to refer to the double performance of Mallarmé's book, and to the double staging of Derrida's paper, and to the partition of my own chapter, *and*, in addition, by way of an almost imperceptible internal fold, to this constantly repeated repetitive doubling of the words: 'the double session'. As the words pass from quotation to title to title to quotation, the movement of reference was anything but paralysed; it was much rather multiplied without end.

Second, in so far as titles, as the word suggests, are always an expression of some legal (though not necessarily legitimate) authority, there was the question of what entitled a title, and, more particularly, of the titular power exerted over writing by such canonic generic titles as 'literature' or 'philosophy'. For those titles, too, at least up to a point, were impossible to avoid, to which Derrida's provisional response, in introducing his talk, was to throw to his audience a series of untranslatable, near-homophonic sub-titles ('L'Antre de Mallarmé', 'L' "Entre" de Mallarmé', 'L'Entre-Deux "Mallarmé"'), each of which, in one way or another, played on the doubleness and uncertainty of what fell *between* – between sounds, places, or meanings (*D*, 207; 181).

Derrida's handout displayed similar attention to between-ness. Of the two anonymous passages it cited, one, by Plato, would most usually be categorised as belonging to philosophy, and the other, by Mallarmé, to literature. But these terms were already uneasy: the extract from Plato was in the form of a fictional dialogue, and thus had at least something to do with one of tradition's longest-established literary genres, while the passage from Mallarmé was ostensibly a theatre review, more akin to a critical, philosophical statement than a piece of literature in its own right. In a way, the two texts were oddly reversible. At the same time, their appearance on the same page in contrasting fonts, as well as emphasising similarity, also drew attention to their differences. Moreover the two quotations were presented not as two exactly counterposed specimens, but asymmetrically, with Plato occupying more space than Mallarmé, and with Mallarmé making inroads on at least some of the space Plato might otherwise have assumed to be his own.

There was on Derrida's part a point to all of this. It marked a refusal to endorse that long-standing conception of 'philosophy' and 'literature' that treats them as adversaries: with the one being devoted to the proper pursuit of original, authentic truth, while the other is forced to make do with those second-hand copies of truth, the false, the fictitious, the inauthentic, and the counterfeit. Admittedly, this was a hierarchy Derrida was not about to reverse, since to do so without dismantling its structure would serve merely to confirm it. Whatever the relationship between Plato and Mallarmé, then, it was evidently not a case of simple opposition. What the format of Derrida's handout raised instead, like the question of the title, was the more complex, more radical question of the problematic structure of all frames, borders, limits, and margins. Could this text by Mallarmé be divided from that by Plato, or was it not somehow part of it? If so, which of the two dominated the other? And what was the nature of the blank space on the page that, stretching beyond the page, surrounded both texts and detached the one from the other, and was also inseparable from every word on the page, irrespective of its provenance?

There was nothing abstract about such questions. Among others, they raised the question of the place or position of Derrida's own paper. Was it merely a footnote to Plato and to Mallarmé? Was it inside Plato's thought or outside it, inside Mallarmé's poetry or outside it? And might it not turn out, as Derrida had argued in the mysterious case of those infelicitous or failed performatives, that what appeared to be outside was in fact already inside (*M*, 387; 325), and that neither inside nor outside could therefore be opposed (as text v. reality, language v. world, essence v. context, necessity v. chance) in the manner assumed to be self-evident by traditional metaphysics along with most conventional literary criticism and theory? That these crucial oppositions were less secure than it seemed was already apparent in Derrida's own opening remarks, and it is no exaggeration to say that everything Derrida describes in 'The Double Session' is demonstrably and necessarily already at work from the outset in his own writing.

What happens in Derrida's paper, so the reader is told, occurs *between* two texts, one presumed to be philosophical, the other to be literary: Plato and Mallarmé.

Why Plato and why Mallarmé?

The significance of Plato for Derrida's project is uncontroversial enough. Derrida's point is that the thing known to readers, critics, and students as 'literature' (the word itself is a relatively recent invention, dating, in its modern sense, in French, from the late eighteenth and, in English, from the early nineteenth century) is not an innocent, neutral object. It is the result of a centuries-long historical process of conceptualisation and institutionalisation on the part of philosophy, among others, beginning as far back as Plato in the fifth century BCE. Whether readers of literature, literary critics, or literary theorists are aware of it or not, argues Derrida, philosophy has programmed, down to the present, much, if not the whole of what it is possible to think under the heading of the term 'literature'. So whether consciously or not, whenever we use the word 'literature', we rely implicitly on a range of sometimes unspoken assumptions that have their origin in the history of philosophy.

'Literature', in other words, is not outside philosophy, but already inside it, not so much its enemy but its secret ally. And in a lengthy footnote glossing the concept of *mimesis* in Plato, which lurks behind all those pale modern counterparts that still dominate literary study: representation, expression, and imitation, Derrida proceeded to set out, in the form of two propositions and six possible consequences, all the various conceptual moves made throughout history by what today is known as literary criticism (*D*, 211–13; 186–7). (It may be noted here in passing that this is why it makes little sense to claim Derridian deconstruction represents a literary approach to philosophical texts. Both the concept of literature and the notion of a specifically literary approach to reading are metaphysical constructs. So if it were true that deconstruction was simply the application of literary methods to philosophical texts, this would merely turn it into yet another, relatively minor episode in the long history of metaphysics.)

During the whole – unfinished – philosophical and historical epoch stretching from Plato to Mallarmé, in which much if not all modern thinking about literature remains deeply embedded, what has dominated throughout, Derrida argues, despite numerous shifts in emphasis or adjustments of one kind or another, is the hierarchically ordered opposition between the intelligible and the sensible: between mind and body, idea and manifestation, signified and signifier, content and form, male and female, and so on. True enough, as Derrida freely acknowledges, the historical system of Platonism should not be confused with Plato's writing, which can be shown already to have the power to deconstruct Platonism, as Derrida shows in the immediately preceding essay in *Dissemination*, 'Plato's Pharmacy' (*D*, 71–197; 63–171).

Plato's historical legacy was nevertheless commanding. So '[w]hat is it', Derrida asks, 'that is decided and kept in place by "Platonism", i.e., directly or indirectly, by the whole history of Western philosophy, including all those anti-Platonisms that have regularly been a feature of it? What is it that is decided and kept in place in ontology or in dialectics despite all the upheavals and revolutions characterising that history?' (*D*, 217; 191).

The answer, according to Derrida, can be summed up in a word: '*Onto-logic* itself [*l'ontologique*: the joining together of *being*, from the Greek word *on*, with *logos*, the Greek word for reason or discourse]: the presumed possibility of a discourse on that which *is*, in other words, of one decidable *logos* deciding upon or making decisions about the *on* (i.e., [in Greek] present-being).' In Plato, read at least in conventional fashion, continues Derrida,

> That which is, i.e. present-being (from which all notions of substance, reality, and all oppositions between matter and form, essence and existence, objectivity and subjectivity, etc., are derived), is distinguished from all semblances, images, or phenomena, etc., i.e., from that which, in presenting it as present-being, doubles it, re-presents it, and thus

replaces and de-presents it. In other words, there is the 1 and the 2, the simple and the double. The double comes *after* the simple; it multiplies it *after the event*. From which it follows (forgive me for rehearsing this yet again) that the image is a belated addition to reality, and representation a kind of after-thought added to the present being presented, in the same way as the imitation is added to the thing, and that which imitates to that which is imitated. There is, then, first: that which is, and goes under the name of 'reality', the thing itself, in flesh and blood, as phenomenologists like to describe it; then, second, imitating the first, come the painting, the portrait, the zographeme [*zographème*: from the Greek, the depiction of a living creature], the inscription or the transcription of the thing itself. Everything here depends absolutely on this discernibility, even if the discernibility is only a numerical one, between that which imitates and that which is imitated. And it goes without saying, of course, according to so-called 'logic' itself, and a deeply enshrined set of equivalences, that what is imitated is more real, more essential, more truthful, etc., than that which imitates. It precedes it, and is superior to it.

(*D*, 217–18; 191; translation modified, and
slightly expanded; author's emphases)

Since Plato, then, notwithstanding all the various shifts in emphasis through history, the 'absolute discernibility between that which is imitated and that which imitates', with the implication that the former always has priority over the latter: this, writes Derrida, has remained constant and unchallenged in the underlying principle of all thinking about literature (*D*, 218; 192; translation modified). Whether an artwork is seen in principle as a genuine approximation of reality, as in traditional criticism, or as a self-conscious copy of reality, as in more recent so-called postmodernist criticism, all this is secondary: so long as the distinction between that which imitates and that which is imitated remains active, and so long as the imitat*ed* is deemed to come first, logically or chrono-logically, as it invariably does, so too, according to Derrida, the metaphysical discourse on art and literature continues to prevail. And what survives as its enduring hallmark of that discourse, whether it is articulated in traditional terms as the conformity between a representation and a thing, or rethought, as it is by Heidegger, according to the more originary figure of unconcealment, is the subordination of all art and literature to the dominant criterion of truth and its corollary, untruth (*D*, 219; 192–3).

This is not to say, however, as some have been too quick to assume, that Derrida in his own writing is somehow willing to ignore, abandon, or relin-quish truth, were this to be possible at all. 'Truth', Derrida insisted in 1997 in conversation with Maurizio Ferraris, 'is not a value one can renounce. The deconstruction of philosophy does not renounce truth, any more, for that matter, than literature does' (*TS*, 10). Throughout his career, unlike others, Derrida was never tempted to give up his commitment to philosophy in the name of some kind of post- or anti-philosophy. What Derrida did envisage, however, was what he called a different or other relation to truth (*TS*, 10). As he pointed out in 1988, in the wake of his exchange with Searle, any careful reading of his texts would show 'that in his work the value of truth (together with all the values that go with it) is never contested or destroyed, but only ever reinscribed in more powerful, more inclusive, more stratified contexts' (*L*, 270; 146; translation modified).

In much the same way, for instance, that the truth claims of Austin's discourse were not undermined by the assertion that the criterion of truth or falsity was not pertinent for an analysis of performatives, so too it hardly followed from Derrida's critique of the claim, going back to Plato, that the very essence of literature was to be mimetic, and was therefore necessarily dominated by the question of truth or untruth, that Derrida's own analysis was an irrational exercise in postmodern fiction-making. On the contrary, it was a searching critique of the pre-emptive dogmatism that commanded thinking about art in the name of (a historically bound, metaphysically determined) truth. As Austin's analysis of performatives showed, with all its limitations, there was in the possibility of writing something necessarily irreducible to questions of truth or untruth. And if this were not the case, it was hard to see how something called truth might come about at all except as divine revelation.

In these circumstances, what, then, 'is' literature?

In introducing that question at the start of his talk, Derrida had first stepped aside, pointing out that the words were already an implicit quotation. They belonged of course to a famously influential book by Sartre, but they were also an unavoidable legacy of the long history of Western metaphysics. In this context, the question was arguably barely a question at all. Its very form already constituted an answer: an answer that assumed, without question, that literature was a 'what?', a 'quid?', a 'something', securely defined, stable, and identical with itself, of which it might then be possible to say what in essence it truly was. There are many different ways of completing the line: 'literature is . . .', suggested Derrida, but what came at the end of the sentence was less important than what was put at the beginning. Once it was taken for granted that there was a thing called 'literature' which 'was', so the whole system of Platonism soon followed, with its tireless subordination of writing to truthful meaning.

Derrida demurred, then, for essential reasons. His refusal to endorse the notion that literature, or art, was identical with itself, and endowed with essential, autonomous being, not only set him apart from many of his contemporaries; it also explains why, contrary to his reputation, Derrida cannot properly be described as a theorist of literature. Though he was sympathetic to the advances made by Russian Formalism and by structuralist literary theory in the attempt to construct a concept of literariness (*Po*, 94–5; 69–70), the fact remained that literature, for Derrida, was not a theorisable object, endowed with essential being, meaning, or purpose. Moreover, if the aim of literary criticism is to specify the meaning(s) of a given work of literature, so too, in his dealings with literary texts, Derrida is anything but a literary critic either.

This was not to say there was not an historical institution called literature. On the contrary, according to Derrida, it was possible to understand that institution only if literature had no proper, ahistorical, ontological essence in the first place. Literature was possible, but it was a possibility that was not determinable in any other way than as a property of *all* language (which was not restricted to one separate, heightened, autonomous, or self-referential state of discourse). What made the institution of literature possible, alongside a number of other, historico-politico-juridical factors, including notably the possibility of democracy, was what he called the becoming-literature, *le devenir-littérature* (*P*, 244; *A*, 229; translation modified) inherent in all language and, in so far as silence is a necessary part of language, in silence too. So if it followed for Derrida that there could be no theory of literature that was not ultimately metaphysical, this was not to say literature was unimportant, quite the reverse, for it meant that the question of literature, to the extent it defied all ontologisation or essentialisation, now became an issue of major philosophical importance. Derrida's refusal to be a literary theorist, then, was no destructive intellectual pirouette: it was a patient and rigorous attempt to release writing in general and so-called literary writing in particular from the legacy of more than two thousand years of metaphysical assumptions.

## II

But how, then, to approach a so-called 'literary' text? How, for instance, to begin reading the prose and poems of Mallarmé?

Commonly known to literary history as a Symbolist, and having the reputation of one of the most difficult writers in the French language, among other reasons because of his idiosyncratic syntax, Mallarmé occupies a pivotal place in the history of poetry and literature. His work marks that crucial moment in literary history when literature became aware of itself not as an established form of self-expression, but as a question. 'Does something like Literature exist?' Mallarmé famously asked an audience of academics, poets, and students in

Oxford, then Cambridge, in 1894; 'other (a convention, in classical times, this was) than the refinement, in view of their burnished expression, of notions, in every area'.[2] Maurice Blanchot, one of Mallarmé's most assiduous post-war readers, giving a decidedly philosophical, not to say Heideggerian inflection to these words, commented as follows: 'When Mallarmé asks, "Does something like Literature exist?", this question is literature itself, it is literature when literature has become the concern for its own essence. Such a question has become unavoidable. What happens by virtue of the fact that we have literature? How do matters stand with regard to being, if one says that "something like Literature exists"?'[3]

As a result, no doubt, of this complex metapoetical turn, Mallarmé's poems throughout the latter part of the twentieth century became a regular focus for theoretical attempts to define modern (or sometimes modernist) writing in general. This was helped, in part, as Derrida notes, by the fact that in philosophical terms Mallarmé counted among the better-informed poets of his generation, having at least some second-hand familiarity with Hegelian dialectics, which made his critical or poetological remarks more easily translatable into modern theoretical language. But though there was consensus about their significance, Mallarmé's poems remained contested property, the object of attempts at appropriation on the part of traditionalist and avant-gardist critics alike, belonging to both political left and right. In the late 1960s, as Derrida was putting the finishing touches to 'The Double Session', matters, if anything, had become more acute. For some commentators Mallarmé remained the supreme aesthete and poetic idealist, while for others he was a dissident anarchist, a revolutionary near-contemporary of Karl Marx, whose writing, appealing to poetic labour rather than to sublime inspiration, exhibited a materialist approach to language, as reflected for instance in Mallarmé's wistful response to a group of toiling workmen entertaining themselves at dusk, which was to remark: 'Perhaps I, too, am a worker.'[4]

While for some his work was esoteric, obscure, and largely written in an alien tongue, to the point of requiring a prose translation into so-called proper French (a task some critics were more than happy to fulfil), for others it provided an exemplary illustration of the inseparability of form and content, and proof that, in literature, the key distinction was no longer between poetry and prose, since Mallarmé's versified and unversified texts displayed the same degree of semantic and syntactic intricacy, but between the essential autonomy of poetic language as such, and the journalistic language of everyday communication. In this respect it was hardly surprising that the work of Mallarmé (and late-nineteenth-century French Symbolist poetry in general) proved an important influence on Roman Jakobson and other Russian Formalists, as well as several like-minded later critics and writers in their endeavour to identify what it was that set so-called poetic language apart from ordinary discourse.

These debates formed another of the contexts within which Derrida's double session was inscribed. Stakes were accordingly high. But as he had with Rousseau in *Of Grammatology*, Derrida began his account of Mallarmé by drawing attention to a little-known, seemingly modest, marginal, off-centre part of the corpus, and with a text that, at first sight, was nothing more than a rather over-elaborate review article. The title of the piece, 'Mimique', without revealing much, did nevertheless suggest that there was something here that had to do with the age-old concept of mimesis. But Derrida insisted it was foolish at best to set up Mallarmean mimicry and Platonic mimesis in opposition. Mallarmé's mime-play was more subtle, oblique, and far-reaching. And it led into a textual labyrinth whose complex machinations it took all Derrida's ingenuity and attention to fine textual and contextual detail to begin to reconstitute.

In the beginning, so to speak, there was, it seems, a mime-show: a silent three-dimensional stage performance, with no speaking parts, without prior script, which Mallarmé describes as already staging a kind of writing, composed and drafted by the mime himself, a writing without words, traced in the air through gesture. But even as it came first, this mime-show also came second. For it was preceded, as far as Mallarmé was concerned, by an earlier writing, in the form of a booklet or script (or libretto), which, in a previous version of Mallarmé's text, under a different title, the writer describes himself as holding in his hands. But this booklet too also came second, and recalled an earlier mime-play that was similarly a writing without words. A never-ending movement was thus set in play, with a series of printed texts referring to a sequence of non-verbal writings which in turn gave rise to a series of written texts, with the result, says Derrida, that, since everything was either a reference back or a reference forward, there was no present in which to anchor any originating present-being of the kind privileged by Platonism. 'There is no Present', Mallarmé famously wrote, 'no – a present does not exist . . .' (*D*, 244; 215).[5]

A similar eclipse or effacing of presence, Derrida argues, was also at work in the stage performance described in 'Mimique'. Within a pair of mysterious quotation marks which divide the text from itself, and install at its centre a double sentence that appears to belong elsewhere, Mallarmé describes the scene thus: 'here preceding, there recalling, in the future, in the past, *under the false appearance of a present*' (*D*, 201, 175; Mallarmé's emphasis; translation slightly modified). In this uncanny present-which-is-not-a-present, then, what Mallarmé has the audience witness is this: the ghostly figure of Pierrot, in characteristic loose white fancy dress and whitened face (whence the earlier mention of the unwritten page embodied by this 'blank phantom' (*D*, 201; 175)), miming in a make-believe present, which is already the repetition of a remembered past, the various preparations made, in the past, by way of planning, in the future, the murder of his deceitful, thieving, violent wife Columbine. Considering but then discarding rope, knife, poison, and gun, Pierrot elects to kill Columbine by tickling her to death, thus marrying, so to speak, extreme pain with extreme pleasure; in this quasi-present re-enacting a future in the past, the mime goes on to show not only how Columbine meets her end, in a sequence mimed frenetically by the only character on stage, Pierrot himself, but also, immediately after, how Pierrot falls under the spell of Columbine and simultaneously, as both himself and not himself, is possessed and overwhelmed (as she is too) by a climactic spasm of pain and pleasure – at which point the murdered Columbine's picture on the wall becomes animated, laughing vengefully at Pierrot's actions, which in turn prompts Pierrot's own demise. Except . . . that if Pierrot dies at the end, the whole performance – Pierrot's memory of how he prepared to kill Columbine, committed the act, and lost his life in the process – cannot be thought to be occurring in any present time or reality, because whoever is repeating the past is either already dead, and lives on only as a ghost, or is not dead, in which case the spectacle to which the audience is invited only ever occurred as a spectral fantasy, unless of course both are simultaneously true and not true, and therefore neither true nor not true, and irreducible to any such opposition. What remains are a series of ghostly enactments, like so many possible or impossible shadows, none of which is graspable in itself as such and attributable to any present-being.

There is more. The booklet or script that Mallarmé claimed once to hold in his hand is not properly present to itself either. It too does not stand alone, in and for itself, but is grafted, attached, adjoined to a series of other texts. The logic is again that of the supplement or prosthesis exploited by Derrida in *Of Grammatology*. At the heart of something seemingly natural, self-identical, and proper, enabling or prolonging its functionality, stands something that is unnatural, other, or improper, with the result that the so-called opposition between natural and unnatural, self and other, proper and improper is called into doubt, and what, by rights, should only be on one side of the equation is found to be already on the other. Such instabilities, Derrida argued, are more common than it may be thought, and represent a grave and irreducible challenge to any concept of self-identity. In Derrida's own entourage, there was soon to be startling confirmation of this originary status of the supplement, inseparable from *différance*, that Derrida formulated in *Of Grammatology* (*G*, 441–5; 313–16). For as readers may know, in the early 1990s Derrida's close friend and associate, the philosopher Jean-Luc Nancy, was the recipient of a heart transplant. As a result of the operation, as he explains in his book *L'Intrus* (*The Intruder*), Nancy was given new life, but only in so far as he found himself now living with the heart of a recently deceased younger woman.[6]

What, wonders Derrida, are the implications of this bodily alteration for the presumed self-identity of the recipient of a graft? Nancy in *L'Intrus* explores many similar questions, all of which derive from the following uncanny paradox: that, as a result of Nancy's surgery, what was now most proper to him, the very heart, so to speak, of his presumed self-identity, was also that which was most improper, radically other to him, and that which, at one and the same time, most powerfully enabled *and* most powerfully threatened his continuing survival. The particular case is exceptional, but the issues it raises are more widespread than might be imagined, and affect more than human or animal lives. It is standard practice, for instance, in growing pears, to graft a cutting from an existing pear tree onto quince rootstock. This allows the grower better to control the size of the future tree, and ensure that it will produce true fruit, the paradox being that the identity of the fruit can only be guaranteed because of the use of non-identical rootstock. Here, too, the tidy opposition between nature and culture, between the natural and the technical, between self and other, becomes infinitely less assured, revealing instead that heterogeneity, admixture, and hybridity are already at work in all presumed identity.

The case is the same with other kinds of texts, as Paul Margueritte's humble script testifies. The story of Pierrot's murder (of Pierrot and by Pierrot) is marked and remarked by numerous explicit or implicit textual allusions. The script cites, for instance, as an epigraph a couplet from Mallarmé's celebrated predecessor, the poet Théophile Gautier (*D*, 231; 203), as well as recalling, more diffusely, the age-old theatrical tradition of the *commedia dell'arte* from which the figures of Pierrot and Columbine are drawn (*D*, 233; 205). As a result, the mime-show is less a place of destination than a space of transit, displacement, and redeparture. And at the end of this chain of allusions set in motion in, around, and by Mallarmé's text stands no point of secure anchorage, no privileged source, text, or historical or other kind of reality capable of arresting the iterative, citational movement of writing. Referral here is deferral, and vice versa; and there is perhaps no better way of understanding *différance*, writes Derrida, than the infinite movement of referral without closure set in motion in and by Mallarmé's text.

Mallarmé's mime-show, as described in his article but also performed by it, therefore represents nothing; it mimes or alludes, says Mallarmé, 'without breaking the glass' (*D*, 234; 206), that is, without interrupting the infinite march of writing and reading. Importantly, these words of Mallarmé are not given in such a way that they dominate the text of which they are a part. On the contrary, they are caught up in a peculiar play of quotation marks and incorporated within what Derrida shows to be a pseudo-quotation, written by Mallarmé himself. The poet's own words, then, prove inseparable from the differantial movement of iterability. They appear here, in 'Mimique', as part of that context; but they equally belong elsewhere. Like the heart beating in the body of Jean-Luc Nancy, they function as a graft, problematising the separation between self and other, here and there, referring back to whence they may have come and forwards to where they will have arrived, without cease.

Their referentiality is similarly multiple: they point not only to the mime-show Mallarmé is allegedly describing, but also to the mime-show his own text is performing, and to the mime-show that the pseudo-quotation itself is enacting, under the false appearance of a quotation. At the heart of the text, of *this* text and all other possible texts, Derrida argues, stands such a potential infinity of writings that it may truly be said that Mallarmé's text (not unlike Nancy's body) has no proper inside, only an improper one, which, if it belongs anywhere, belongs equally well outside. But having no proper inside, it cannot logically have a proper outside either. But this, writes Derrida, is what 'Mimique' 'is' (or 'is' not), beyond or before any present-being: 'a referring without referent, without primary or ultimate unity, a ghost that is the ghost of no flesh, wandering the earth without a past, without death, without birth or presence either' (*D*, 234; 206; translation modified).

Students of literary theory are of course well accustomed to the idea that texts, literary or otherwise, are constituted in dialogue with other literary or non-literary texts. No text stands alone without referring to a whole library of others. This is what since the mid-1960s has come to be known as intertextuality (and it is worth noting that via the pioneering work of Mikhail Bakhtin intertextuality is another late offshoot of Russian Formalism). In emphasising the extent to which 'Mimique' is part of a potentially infinite network of writings, how far, it may be wondered, is Derrida reverting to the classic Formalist, proto-structuralist notion of language as a prison-house where words are thought simply to refer to other words, in the absence of any connection other than a conventional one with the so-called outside world of history, society, or politics? A strongly held prejudice has it, of course, that Derrida (and so-called deconstruction in general) is interested only in textual play, rather than, say, the historico-political conditions of production, distribution, or consumption of actual works. By way of support for the claim, critics have sometimes thought it enough to cite a phrase that first appeared in *Of Grammatology* in 1967, where Derrida wrote: '*Il n'y a pas de hors-texte*', a sentence usually, if problematically, translated into English as: '*There is nothing outside of the text*' (*G*, 227; 158; author's emphasis).

The context of Derrida's remark makes clear what is at stake here. For Derrida is *not* saying that biography, history, politics, and so on, do not exist, and that words, referring to other words, are the only things that matter. *Nor* is he claiming that everything in the world is mediated through words, and that therefore, whether we like it or not, the only access to so-called reality is by way of the textual archive (though there are things, like the life of Rousseau, that are only available to the reader largely through what Rousseau himself wrote, which has to be taken into account). *Nor* is he asserting, as did the semiologist and critic Roland Barthes, following on from Saussure, that linguistics provides the best available methodology for understanding how history, culture, literature, even everyday life are endowed with meaning. These were all positions Derrida, from the outset, had subjected to severe critical scrutiny. In reading Derrida's formula, then, it is essential to recall that *différance*, together with what Derrida calls (arche-)writing and what he addresses here as 'text', is not part of a theory of language in either the conventional or even the Saussurean sense. The claim that '*Il n'y a pas de hors-texte*' (which might equally be translated as 'nothing is extra-textual' or 'text knows no bounds') is part of Derrida's fundamental argument that there is nothing which is not affected by *différance*, iterability, and the trace as non-present remainder. It does not mean everything may be reduced to language, but that, where (arche-)writing is concerned, there is no inside nor outside, since any such division is itself dependent on the tracing or marking Derrida, for strategic reasons, calls writing. As he suggests in 'Signature event context', it would be impossible even to conceive of experience (i.e. time, space, perception, memory, the unconscious, self and other, etc.) without recourse to some concept of (arche-)writing in so far as 'there is no experience of *pure* presence, but only chains of differential marks' (*M*, 378; 318). Whether inside language (in the conventional sense) or outside it, all is a matter of differential articulation and repetition-as-difference. And as far as 'Mimique' is concerned, the lesson was clear enough: no inside, no outside, no discernible distinction, therefore, between that which may be thought *to imitate*, and that which may be thought *to be imitated*, no mimesis or anti-mimesis, and no truth or untruth dominating the text.

Instead, as far as 'Mimique' went, there remained the hymen, which the writer set between pseudo-quotation marks, as though to put both the word and the thing at a distance from itself, at the very moment it was ostensibly being presented to the reader, thereby citing it as a word or thing that was both itself and something other than itself, or, while being itself, was also not quite itself. 'Here then', wrote Mallarmé, describing the scene: '"The scene illustrates but the idea, not an effective action, in a hymen (from which proceeds the Dream), dissolute but sacred, between desire and fulfilment, perpetration and memory: here preceding, there recalling, in the future, in the past, *under the false appearance of a present*. Thus operates the Mime, whose acting is limited to a perpetual allusiveness without breaking the glass: it installs, thus, a medium, purely, of fiction"' (*D*, 201; 175; translation modified).

As Derrida points out, and indeed as Mallarmé's text indicates in the story it tells of Pierrot's unhappy marriage and even more unhappy divorce, and in the use it makes of quotation marks, simultaneously coupling and uncoupling this text with another, the word hymen *both* means a wedding (Hymen in Greek mythology is the god of marriage, pictured carrying a torch and a veil, i.e., something which penetrates and something which resists) *and* is the name given to the virginal membrane partially closing the external orifice of the vagina, which has to be breached if there is to be heterosexual congress. In either sense, what 'hymen' names is what goes or comes *between*: what conjoins *and* holds apart. In 'Mimique' the two meanings are different but go together, as though to suggest that what hymen in Mallarmé's text inscribes, as a coming together and a staying apart, is the word hymen itself.

But the word not only alluded to itself, it also referred to the strange suspension (neither real nor unreal, true nor untrue) characterising both the mime-show witnessed by Mallarmé and the poet's description or re-enactment of the play, i.e. 'Mimique' itself. Various separate but cohabiting layers of sense jostle equally for attention. Meaning is not finalised, but suspended. It hovers, so to speak, between terms. What counts here, though, for Derrida, is not in itself the serendipitous convergence of two contrary meanings within the same word, but the syntax that, in this specific text, affirms and exploits the strange marriage between the two senses of the word hymen, which comes to signify itself and its opposite, twice over. Derrida goes on to analyse the semantic and syntactic mobility of Mallarmé's text, which, he argues, far from being a special feature of Mallarmean poetic language as such, though it is infinitely potentialised in Mallarmé's hands, is a characteristic common to textuality in general.

The movement by which meaning is suspended, or deferred, or affected with improbable forms of reversibility, Derrida in 'The Double Session' calls it: the undecidable. The word was to have a significant future and soon became inseparable from the popular image of deconstruction. Derrida conceded, however, in 'The Double Session' that it was used only provisionally, and by way of analogy (*D*, 240; 211). It corresponded, simply enough, to an attempt to think the writing of Mallarmé outside of the binary opposition of truth or untruth as programmed by Platonism. Derrida insisted that the undecidable was not in itself a theme, or something that governed thematic meaning in a text, though it might manifest itself in that way. As far as 'Mimique' was concerned, its effects might be measured more closely by examining again the pseudo-quotation marks used by Mallarmé at the centre of his text. The two sentences contained within inverted commas, suggests Derrida, are part of Mallarmé's text while themselves remaining 'under glass'; they are brought into focus, but remain beneath a veil. They are put at a distance from the reader, in other words, but without the import of that distance being properly determined. Did the status of those words as a quotation lend them greater authority, or diminish their status by setting them at arm's length, or somehow both? What followed from the realisation that the idiosyncratic syntax of the quotation quickly identified it as a pseudo-quotation, penned in fact by the purported author of the text? If it was implicitly signed: Mallarmé, why were the two sentences presented as a quotation at all? So many unanswerable questions, then, all requiring an interpretative decision, but in the process making any decision impossible. And was what Mallarmé writes or cites within this parenthesis-that-is-not-entirely-a-parenthesis to be taken as true or untrue, or might it not be that the use of quotation marks suspends or defers that very question? If *hymen* can mean both conjunction and separation, in the same way that the word *between* serves to join together two nouns, adjectives, prepositions, adverbs, or verbs, while also keeping them apart, how might it be possible to select one of the positions rather than the other? Is one not forced to refuse the alternative, and opt for a third possibility: not the one nor the other, but both – and neither.

The undecidable, in this way, enacts the ghostly possibility of an impossible third term: neither one nor the other, nor any synthesis of these two available positions, nor indeed a position at all. As far as 'Mimique' is concerned, its emblem was Pierrot himself: comic but also sad, silent but also eloquent, the perpetrator but also the victim, male but also female, himself but also another, alive but also dead: a spectre, dressed in white, like the unwritten page. Rather than being reducible to any position, then, the undecidable affirms and reaffirms the ineluctable movement of spacing – of writing – that is logically prior to one and the other, which it contains and outstrips. In Derrida's terms, undecidability is therefore decidedly *not* peaceful neutrality, or some courteous, liberal tolerance of diversity of opinion. Its more radical connection is with the question of framing adumbrated by Derrida at the start of his talk. Frames, like contexts, are indispensable and inevitable; yet they are always and necessarily fragile. For where does a frame begin or end? Is not an absence of frame already a frame, and does not the presence of one frame always invite the possibility of fitting another frame, in the same way that it is always possible to keep on adding quotation marks? All framing is affected by such interminability; and what seems to count most of all is not the presence of this or that frame, but the fact that one is never enough, that to frame an object is also by the same gesture to open it to the possibility of another frame, and so on, ad infinitum, with no single frame ever being in a position to bring to a close the ongoing predicament of framing.

The undecidable operates in much the same way. It marks a movement in the text that exceeds all static themes or theses. As such, it is something that is always already in suspense, to the point of reversing itself at times into its very opposite, according to what Derrida elsewhere, borrowing the example from the psychoanalysis of Sigmund Freud, calls the argument of the girdle (see *Gl*, 252–4b; 226–7b). This had its origin in a case cited by Freud in his 1927 paper on 'Fetishism', exploring the process, not unlike prosthetic substitution, by which objects that are not in themselves explicitly sexual, including parts of the body like the nose or the foot, or clothing that sits close to the body like underwear or footwear, may come to be invested with sexual significance.[7]

The fetish, Freud contends, is best understood as a substitute or replacement standing in for a missing object. Its status therefore is almost exactly that of a sign. In fetishism, according to Freud, the identity of the missing object to which the fetish refers is nonetheless clear: it is invariably a penis, albeit a very particular penis, he suggests, which is the one presumed to have originally belonged to the mother, but which, visibly, has been removed leaving her castrated. Though the fetishist might be fully aware, intellectually, of the anatomical differences between the sexes, Freud argues, the fetish nonetheless allows him (fetishists in Freud are almost invariably male) to cling obstinately, against all reason, to the phantasy that things are otherwise.

By way of illustration of this peculiar logic of duplicity and compromise, Freud cites one particularly ingenious individual given to wearing, as a fetish, a genital sheath or girdle (Freud's English translator, James Strachey, calls it an athletic support belt), similar in design to a pair of early twentieth-century bathing trunks. And Freud explains:

> This piece of clothing entirely concealed genitals and genital difference alike. According to what emerged in analysis, what it meant for the patient was *both* that women were castrated *and* that they were *not* castrated, while also allowing the assumption that men were castrated too, since all these possibilities could equally well be hidden under the girdle, which had begun life, during his childhood, as a fig-leaf seen on a statue. A fetish of this sort, doubly bound together from contradictory ideas is of course especially durable.[8]

What interested Derrida in this example was not the implicit notion that sexual difference between men and women might be seen in oppositional terms, between the presence of prominent genital equipment on the one hand, and a corresponding lack of such equipment on the other, a traditional masculinist or phallogocentric assumption, as he calls it, that Derrida firmly rejected. What is however noteworthy is the strangely reversible double meaning of the fetish. As its origin in the classical fig-leaf suggests, there is here something that stretches far back into cultural history, and points to a canonic, radically inescapable condition of all textuality. For to cover the genitalia of a statue with a fig-leaf is a highly ambiguous gesture. For even as it obscures what it is felt inappropriate for the audience to see, it also, by that selfsame token, draws the audience's attention to what it is designed to conceal, making it more noticeable still, and even perhaps reproducing and exaggerating its visual aspect. The unintentional but irresistible duplicity that then accrues can quickly seem ubiquitous. When, for instance, I cover my lips with my hand while making an uncomplimentary remark in someone's presence, does my hand conceal the fact that I am speaking inappropriately, as I may intend, or does it not, by emphasising it, reveal the fact that I am doing something I consider improper? By reinforcing an area where I feel particularly open to attack, am I protecting myself or simply conceding my vulnerability? As politicians have sometimes discovered to their cost, the more I attempt to cover up a crime, the more clues I leave behind, increasing the risk not only that the original crime will be uncovered, but all my subsequent malpractice too which rather than mitigating the offence serves merely to make it more culpable. And the more I seek in public to justify a controversial decision, the more unjustifiable it becomes. The more I strain in one direction, then, just like Freud's fetishist, the more I find myself being pushed into the opposite one, without it being possible ultimately to decide the true (or untrue) sense of my behaviour.

Both inside literature and outside literature, if indeed such a frontier can be policed at all, examples of such contrary logic are many. They have particular currency in psychoanalysis, and were what led Freud to conclude, for instance, that the unconscious was oblivious to contradiction, so easy was it for the dreaming or fantasising mind to allow the same word, symbol, or symptom at the very same time to present diametrically opposed, antagonistic meanings; and this was how, with the use of the selfsame girdle, and with remarkable economy of effort, Freud's bather was able to entertain as one no fewer than four incompatible ideas: that women were simultaneously castrated and *not* castrated, and men likewise. Such convictions are perhaps not common, but even if it was found only once, it would still be necessary to account for its possibility. This Derrida was able to do by arguing that the reversibility of meaning found in the fetish followed logically from the proposition that meanings were not rooted in transcendent truths, but in *différance* and iterability, in the constant reframing of meaning(s) within repeatedly different contexts. As a result, meaning was always the product of a precarious balance between force and counter-force, and what might seem to signify one thing in a given context would always risk implying its very opposite elsewhere, without contradiction, and without synthesis. Derrida indeed argues as much in *Glas*, where exactly this oscillating motion of binding and counterbinding is put to work under the rubric of a generalised economy of the fetish.

Faced with writing like that of Mallarmé, in which such reversals of meaning and slippages of syntax were prominent and inescapable, how to proceed? This was the main burden of Derrida's second session, which began with a further detour through recent reception of Mallarmé's poetry, in particular with a consideration of the work of the critic Jean-Pierre Richard, the author of an imposing and highly influential doctoral thesis entitled *L'Univers imaginaire de Mallarmé* (*Mallarmé's Imaginative Universe*).[9] This was a remarkable achievement, painstaking and all-encompassing, deeply indebted to phenomenology and its methods. What Richard had sought to do, in this, as in other comparable studies, was to describe in detail the mental landscape inhabited by the poet and reconstruct the writer's existential project as it realised itself in and through writing. The specific unit of analysis of this approach was the poetic theme: mobile but unified, concrete but intelligible, the literary embodiment, so to speak, of the poet's presence in the world.

There are, of course, many different kinds of literary criticism for which the concept of theme is of pivotal importance and many different ways of defining what constitutes a theme. But in the whole of literary criticism, as it is customarily taught or practised, there are probably few more basic concepts, and many are the students in secondary school or high school whose first encounter with literary criticism will have been in the form of a requirement to identify the so-called main themes of a text. Essay questions of this kind proliferate wherever literature is taught: 'What, in your view', say the examination papers, 'are the main themes in *Hamlet* (*Macbeth*, *Middlemarch*, or *Ulysses*)?' In comparison, Richard's critical methods are highly sophisticated. A common assumption shared nevertheless by Richard's criticism and other, more humble or workaday forms of literary commentary is that the work of writing consists in putting into place, positioning, or positing thematic meaning(s). Etymologically, this is what a *theme* is; the word is from the Greek, and derives from a root meaning: to put, set, place, or lay down, which is how *thema*, in Greek, via Latin, comes to mean: a proposition, i.e. a putting forward and setting down. Everything hinges therefore on this ability to identify and recognise (textual) places. But what Derrida's 'Double Session' shows is the ineradicable fragility of all such positions or places, which continually find themselves neither inside nor outside, never simply here nor simply there. If iterability is to be taken seriously, Derrida argues, it can but call into question the very possibility of thematic readings.

The work of Richard represented an important test case. But what was more fundamentally at issue for Derrida was the possibility of thematic criticism in so far as it was characteristic of modern literary criticism in general. Thematic criticism, Derrida maintained, is what is always 'at work whenever the aim is to determine a meaning throughout a text, to decide what it is, i.e. that it is single, and meaningful, and that as meaning it is posed, and posable or transposable as such, as a theme' (*D*, 276; 245; translation modified). Richard's particular method, Derrida acknowledged, was flexible and robust, and keenly sensitive to textual nuance. But there was, by definition, an underlying difficulty such as to threaten any attempt to nominate stable, recognisable, and identifiable themes in a text. For any text, Richard himself concedes, is necessarily a fabric or network, in which meaning is produced, from one context to another, by virtue of an interplay of difference and repetition. That movement it is, of course, which allows readers to identify themes. But if so, the theme is *not* what it pretends to be, i.e., a constant and recognisable nucleus of meaning, but at best only a secondary thematic effect. If the theme does exist as the unchanging core of meaning it purports to be, Derrida points out, it certainly could not, and would not appear as such in any text (*D*, 282; 249–50).

Thematic criticism, then, rests on a more or less violent act of naming; and it comes as no surprise that thematic criticism in general tends to name in a text what it can most readily place there, or for which it can most readily find a place. This usually means extracting from a text, in reductive fashion, those motifs that lend themselves to translation or transposition into critical commentary. And it also means, argues Derrida, that thematic criticism is forced to disregard those many moments, particularly frequent in the poems of Mallarmé, when words, like *hymen*, in addition to naming the object to which they refer, and alongside the numerous metaphorical or other meanings with which those objects are invested, also do something remarkable and insistent, which is to refer to their own performance, without this ever turning into a theme as such.

Towards the end of his double talk, Derrida reverts, then, without ever having properly left it, to that strange logic of the fold with which he began, and which had instantiated itself in the way in which his own talk, spread over a double session, had ended up not only calling itself 'The Double Session', but in the process exploring, as in the figure of Pierrot, the numerous spectral implications of doubleness. Elsewhere, too, there are countless examples of the movement by which, in addition to everything else they do, words allow themselves to be folded back on themselves, performing or enacting their own reading or writing, referring to themselves, as it were, in an infinite circle without beginning or end, and without this process of abyssal reflection ever touching any bottom or reaching any foundation. A canonic example of this drama may be found in Mallarmé's famous last poem, 'Un Coup de dé jamais n'abolira le hasard' ('A Throw of the Dice Will Never Abolish Chance'), in which, among others, and again spread over a double page, in various carefully calculated self-referring visual configurations, a story (without story) is told, involving a shipwreck, in which like the poet the master on board goes down with his ship, plunging to the bottomless depths of the ocean amidst crashing waves foaming white upon the blanked-out page.[10]

But more humdrum scenarios serve equally well. Mallarmé had, for instance, a great fondness for the fans that were a customary part of female attire in the drawing rooms of his day, even to the point of producing a series of brief poems, each of which was inscribed, line by line, on the wings of a fan; and the writer did something similar too with postal addresses and Easter eggs.[11] In such instances, the text of the poem was tied, at least provisionally, to a particular material context. To read the poem it was enough to open the fan, and, when it was finished, close it. This may seem like a rather esoteric parlour game. But it was not without significance. What it showed was that, in addition to all the other things they may or may not signify, fans in Mallarmé were also a kind of material embodiment of the folding and unfolding of the poem, which always occurred, in the blink of an eye, so to speak, before meaning was able to settle in any place. To encounter the word *fan* in Mallarmé, before any possible thematic meaning(s), and always in addition to any such meaning(s), then, was to be faced with a silent, redoubled movement of deferral and referral, for as the fan opened and closed, so did the poem, and vice versa, without end (*D*, 283; 251–2).

Caution needs to be exercised, however, in describing such writing effects as instances of textual self-reflexivity or literary self-consciousness, for reasons Derrida underlines in 'The Double Session' (*D*, 302–3; 270–1). What such formulations imply, at the very least as a kind of aspirational goal, is the possibility of some final or ultimate coincidence between object and reflection. To attribute the folds and reduplications of Mallarmé's writing to textual self-reflexivity or self-consciousness runs the obvious risk of rethematising them as attributes of the poet's mental universe. This was to forget that between the opening of a text and its subsequent possible meaning(s) there was always a necessary and irreducible margin which meant that all possibility of coincidence or identification between text and meaning was unavailable from the outset.[12]

In the same way that the line of the horizon draws all that falls within it into the field of vision without itself ever being visible as such, so there is a margin or excess implicit in all writing, Derrida explains, that can never be captured as a theme, and without which it would not even be possible to begin naming or describing themes at all. This marked a crucial intervention on Derrida's part. It showed that it was not enough simply to posit meaning as always already plural, as for instance Roland Barthes had contended in his book *S/Z*, written at almost exactly the same time as 'The Double Session', and driven, within the context of a (post-Formalist) concern with the specificity of poetic or literary language, by the need to distinguish between different regimes of meaning, which Barthes famously called the *lisible*, the readable, and the *scriptible*, the writeable.[13]

This polysemic coexistence of multiple meanings in a text promoted by Barthes, though obviously an improvement on other modes of reading, did not however go far enough for Derrida. By treating everything as always already meaningful, it could in fact account neither for the emergence nor for the suspension of meaning, and made it impossible to understand how any text, rather than being a static formal convention, might constitute an event: singular, unpredictable, and inexhaustible. For Derrida, this was an essential require-ment, and the reason why it was imperative, he argued, to think outside of the horizon of meaning. Borrowing a word from Mallarmé, Derrida gave this excess of meaning that was always both *more than* and *otherwise than* the plurality of meaning, a name that soon became another of Derrida's signature terms. That word was: *dissemination*. Referring to Mallarmé's usage of the words *fan*, *book*, or *dancer*, each of which functions in self-referential fashion, Derrida explained as follows:

> It is now necessary for us to attempt to write the word *dissemination*.
> And to explain why one always has difficulty following [i.e.
> understanding *and* coming after as a critic] the text of Mallarmé.
> For if, beyond these textual instances, there is no thematic unity or total
> meaning that might be reappropriated within, say, the imagination,
> intentionality, or lived experience, then the text is no longer the
> expression or representation (successful or not) of any *truth* that might
> be said to be diffracted or gathered up in the polysemy of literature. This
> hermeneutic concept of *polysemy* needs therefore to be replaced by that
> of *dissemination*.     (*D*, 294; 262; translation modified)

Dissemination, then, is not a property of meaning, which it both precedes and exceeds. '*Dissemination*, in the end', writes Derrida, 'is not bound to meaning and cannot be gathered together in any definition' (*Po*, 61; 44; translation modified). Indeed, throughout 'The Double Session', reflecting on the word(s) 'between [*entre*]' that the paper takes as its emblem, Mallarmean writing is articulated by Derrida, first, as a syntax before it is a semantics (*D*, 206; 180), then, second, and more radically still, as that opening or spacing between the syntactic and the semantic, which as such is irreducible to the semantic and the syntactic alike (*D*, 252; 222). It manifests itself in Mallarmé's texts, then, not only at the level of the word, but also as a differential (or differantial) movement of phonemes, graphemes, and letters. In so doing, it infinitises the text. Which is why, for Derrida, there is nothing negative about dissemination. On the contrary, it is an absolutely affirmative gesture:

> Following a schema tested out in respect of '*entre* [*between*]', the quasi 'meaning' of dissemination is the impossible return to any reassembled or refurbished unity of meaning, and the barred progress of any such *reflection*. But is dissemination, for all that, the *loss* of any truth of this kind, the *negative* prohibition preventing access to any signified of this sort? Far from accrediting the notion that some virgin substance precedes or controls it, dispersing itself or making itself unavailable in what would be a second negative moment, dissemination *affirms* the always already divided generation of meaning. Dissemination – lets it drop, in advance.     (*D*, 299–300; 268; translation modified)

The impossibility of beginning; the irreducibility but unsaturability of context; the limits of onto-logic, literary theory, and criticism; mime-play without mimesis; writing without inside or outside; the undecidable; dissemination; affirmation – this was the course Derrida plotted in those two weeks early in 1969, as 'The Double Session' folded and unfolded its rethinking of what, obstinately enough, still called itself literature. It was a project Derrida continued to pursue with extraordinary persistence and inventiveness in the years to come.

For its part 'The Double Session' was Derrida's final contribution to the self-styled avant-garde project of the *Tel Quel* group. Their association had lasted little more than five years, and by 1971, unconvinced by the group's increasingly theatrical turn to Maoism, and enjoying a more nuanced understanding of Mao's Cultural Revolution through his friendship with Lucien Bianco (*OCC*, iii), Derrida had begun clearly to distance himself from the strange blend of dogmatism and weathervane opportunism the journal had now come to represent.

## The law of genre

Following publication of *Dissemination* in 1972, Derrida continued to set the agenda for a new style of encounter between philosophy and so-called literary

texts. 1974 was the year of *Glas*, one of Derrida's most far-reaching achievements, which considerations of length make it impossible for me to explore
further here.[14] The book was accompanied by a growing number of essays
and papers dealing with philosophers such as Nietzsche, Kant, and Heidegger,
with the psychoanalytic theory of Freud and Lacan, and with various literary
texts too, including notably the work of the poet Francis Ponge and, perhaps
most significantly of all for Derrida himself, the literary critic, philosopher, and
novelist, Maurice Blanchot.

Maurice Blanchot (1907–2003) is without doubt one of the most original
and influential writers of the whole post-war era in France. But in the eyes of
many, even into the 1980s and 1990s, he remained a shadowy and intimidating presence. Derrida's efforts to reclaim the writer's work for contemporary
thought began in 1976 with a long piece entitled 'Pas' (meaning both: steps
and nots), written partly in response to Blanchot's book *Le Pas au-delà* (*The
Step Not Beyond*), written entirely in fragments, which had appeared three
years before.[15] But it was not only the attention of French readers Derrida was
concerned to capture. I have already mentioned *Deconstruction and Criticism*,
the book that would launch Derrida's American career as a writer on literary
texts, to which he contributed an essay on Blanchot's 1948 story *L'Arrêt de
mort* (*Death Sentence*), which had only recently been translated into English
(*P*, 111–203; *DC*, 75–176).[16] The same year, at an international conference (on
'Genre') jointly sponsored by the University of Strasbourg and Johns Hopkins
University, it was again on a work of fiction by Blanchot, the story *La Folie du
jour* (*The Madness of the Day*), that Derrida chose to speak. And throughout
the 1970s, there were seminars on Blanchot both in Paris and at Yale, with the
material on *La Folie du jour* also forming part of the seminar and lecture series
entitled *Donner le temps* (*Given Time*), the early part of which, on the gift in
various philosophical, anthropological, and literary texts, including the prose
poems of Baudelaire, was published in 1991.[17]

In 1986, all four essays on Blanchot had been brought together in French
with a brief introduction under the title *Parages*, a book that, strangely enough,
has never been translated into English as a single volume, though two of the
essays it contains first appeared in English translation (and one other in Italian),
establishing a pattern that would continue for the remainder of Derrida's career,
and which increasingly bound his thinking to the question (and problems) of
translation. Admittedly, *Parages* was intentionally a somewhat disparate collec-
tion, in part because Derrida was unwilling to write about Blanchot in the name
of philosophy pure and simple and thereby endorse (and enforce) the political
and institutional divide between the philosophical and the literary (which was
not to say they were reducible to the same thing), in part too because it was

never his goal to produce something resembling an exhaustive theoretical discourse bearing on Blanchot's work as a whole. It was essential, too, in Derrida's eyes, in addressing some of Blanchot's singular texts, to remain faithful to the particular settings in which his readings of Blanchot had seen the light of day, which were for the most part closely related to Derrida's responsibilities as a teacher, even if (or precisely because) what Blanchot wrote was decidedly resistant to the communication of any *ex cathedra* lesson, doctrine, or message (*P*, 9–16).

In later years, Derrida continued to work and write on Blanchot, publishing in 1996 a long commentary on Blanchot's brief 1994 semi-autobiographical narrative, *L'Instant de ma mort* (*The Instant of My Death*), in which the writer recounted his near-execution by firing squad in 1944, with Derrida's essay 'Demeure' subsequently appearing, in English translation, side by side with Blanchot's story four years later.[18] In February 2003, it fell to Derrida to deliver the eulogy at Blanchot's funeral,[19] while a month later, together with Jean-Luc Nancy, another long-standing admirer of Blanchot, he was responsible for the closing plenary at the first major conference on Blanchot's work to be held in France (*P*, 269–300). Derrida's relationship with predecessors and contemporaries was often purposefully divided, and he displayed a remarkable ability to combine a relentless commitment to critical vigilance with an always generous, at times effusive sense of indebtedness. Such was the relationship, he once observed, albeit in very different ways, that bound him to the thought of both Heidegger and Levinas; it was however his intellectual friendship with Blanchot, he added, that suffered fewest tremors, and experienced least in the way of peaks and troughs (*HF*, 106).[20]

Perhaps Derrida's most accessible text on Blanchot for readers unfamiliar with the writer's work is the paper 'The Law of Genre', presented at the 1979 Strasbourg conference mentioned above (*P*, 233–66; *A*, 223–52). Derrida's intervention was once again a response to a specific theoretical context, which is best summed up by the word *genre* itself, which, in French, more so than in English, and without necessarily discriminating between them, means: a *genus* (i.e. a class, a category, or a family, like humanity in general, which may be divided further into its component species); a *genre* (in the sense of a literary or other kind of genre, consisting of a corpus of texts that share a set of common features); and *gender* (the initial meaning of which was linguistic or grammatical, but which came to be used increasingly, in the 1970s, and particularly in English, as a way of conceptualising the socio-cultural representation of sexual differences). The range of meanings covered by the word was very wide; but in each of these sub-genres of the word *genre*, as Derrida would go on to show, everything hinged, first, on the possibility of articulating a type of system of types, kinds, or sorts, based on hierarchical differentiation (not to say discrimination), and, second, on the possibility of allocating individuals (whether people, texts, or words) to one or other of the categories for which they were eligible.

The concept of genre governs a vast number of different areas of inquiry. But it has particular relevance, often of a very practical kind, for the study of texts. In the literary field, genre theory has long been an important strand of investigation. Already much of the early work of the Russian Formalists was carried out in relation to particular poetic or narrative genres like the traditional folk-tale; but there have been a host of other empirical or thematically based studies since. The reasons for this are not hard to fathom. One of the powerful attractions of work on literary or other types of genre is that it offers the possibility of reconciling formal or structural perspectives with historical ones. An inquiry into the Hollywood musical, for instance, or 1930s Hollywood gangster films, allows the researcher both to consider the narrative or other conventions typical of the genre, and to plot the rise and fall of the genre within a specific socio-historical, economic, or industrial context.

Invariably, insurmountable theoretical issues arise. These mainly have to do with the difficulty of rigorous differentiation. Imponderables proliferate. Where, for instance, does the line pass between one genre and the next? When does formulaic repetition turn to parody or pastiche? What is the relation between repetition and innovation? What traits are properly generic, and which are merely circumstantial? What criteria are primary and what are merely secondary? In specifying what a given genre is allowed to include or exclude, what norms are being invoked or imposed, and by what authority? And if a text is attributed to one genre rather than another, what are the consequences for its interpretation?

Genre theory, then, is no minor genre within literary or film theory and criticism. It reached to the heart of the question: what is literature? that Derrida had not ceased pursuing since 'The Double Session', not, of course, with a view to supplying an answer, but in order to retrace the long history of the question and analyse the assumptions implicit within it. In 1979, as far as France was concerned, the debate took a step forward, in at least two ways. First, the philosophers Philippe Lacoue-Labarthe and Jean-Luc Nancy, Derrida's conference hosts in Strasbourg, and strong supporters of his work, had the previous year, under the title *L'Absolu littéraire* (*The Literary Absolute*), published an important anthology of relatively unavailable (and in some instances hitherto untranslated) critical and philosophical texts from the period 1798–1800, written principally by that celebrated group of innovative writers known to posterity as the Jena Romantics: the two Schlegel brothers, Friedrich and August

Wilhelm, and Novalis.[21] Not only had the concept of literature in its modern sense largely been invented in those texts, Lacoue-Labarthe and Nancy argued; it was that the theory of literature the Jena Romantics devised was largely a theory of literary genres, with Romantic poetry taking on the exceptional mantle of the genre designed 'to reunite all separate genres of poetry, and put poetry in touch with both philosophy and rhetoric' according to the famous Fragment 116 from the *Athenäum*, the key journal edited by the Schlegel brothers during that short but turbulent period.[22]

There was a second body of work that was relevant too. Since its beginnings in the 1950s and 1960s, structuralist literary theory had by the 1970s significantly mutated and split off into various different, often competing branches or sub-disciplines. Perhaps the most important of these second-generation avatars of structuralist theory, associated with the journal *Poétique*, founded in 1970, was the work of Gérard Genette and Tzvetan Todorov, which had by now turned itself into a fully fledged theory of narrative, or narratology as it became known, and which concentrated principally, though not exclusively, on literary narrative. By the latter half of the decade, narratology too had begun to turn its attention to genre, most pertinently, for Derrida's purposes, in the shape of an article by Genette first published in 1977 and reissued as a slim volume two years later under the title *Introduction à l'architexte* (*The Architext: an Introduction*).[23] In the essay, which retraced the complex, shifting history of thinking about genre from its beginnings in Aristotle's *Poetics* through seventeenth-century classicism, eighteenth-century aesthetics, and German Romanticism to the more scientific, language-based disquisitions of the present, Genette sought to provide a more reliable foundation for genre theory, which he did by carefully distinguishing, as earlier writers in his view had often failed to do, between what he called modes and genres. A mode, according to Genette, was a non-literary or pre-literary, formal property of language: did a poet speak or write in his or her own name (pure narration), or delegate all speech to third-person characters (dramatic imitation), or alternate between the two (mixed narration)? Genre, on the other hand, was defined as a specifically literary, historically situated realisation of an underlying mode: mixed narration, he argued, at a given point in history, had given rise to the genre of the novel, which in turn, on the basis of the same mode, had spawned an ever more bewildering number of sub-genres (the epistolary novel or novel by letters; the Gothic novel; the detective novel, etc.), or sub-sub-genres (the hard-boiled detective novel; the *noir* thriller; the country-house whodunit), and so on.

Genette's enterprise was a sustained attempt at clarification, redescription, and rearticulation. As such, Derrida agreed, it represented significant progress in an increasingly confused area of literary theory. In other ways, however,

Genette's approach was anything but new. It amounted to a reintroduction of a long-established philosophical distinction: that which separates the natural or transcendental, on the one hand, and the historico-cultural or empirical, on the other. Modes referred to the formal conditions of possibility governing the structure and identity of the particular historical objects called genres which, in turn, were governed or commanded by ahistorical modes. But how secure was Genette's distinction? Was it not an inevitable consequence of *différance* and iterability, Derrida argued, that, however essential it might be for philosophy in general, the opposition between the transcendental and the empirical could not always be rigorously maintained, and ran the risk of contamination, displacement, slippage – which philosophy owed it to itself to attempt to measure?

Derrida's Strasbourg paper was in three parts: a preamble; a demonstration; and an illustration. But none of these generic moments was in fact quite what it seemed. The talk began, nevertheless, with an object lesson in the problem it was addressing. '*Ne pas mêler les genres*': these were Derrida's opening words (*P*, 233; *A*, 223). From the outset, a certain context imposed itself, if only, for instance, because Derrida's audience would recognise these to be words in French. But that context left much still to be determined. For there were several different ways of interpreting (and translating) the phrase, according to the mode of speech, discursive genre, or type of presentation to which it was attributed. That opening phrase, Derrida suggested, might be taken as a neutral statement, as found in a dictionary, with the verb *mêler* being used as an ordinary infinitive: 'not to mix genres'. But alternatively, and simultaneously, according to French grammar (as illustrated by the standard formula: *ne pas cracher*, no spitting), they could be taken as a kind of universal imperative: 'No mixing of genres allowed.' In either case, was Derrida using these words to express a personal opinion, or mentioning them as an example of what they represented?

Derrida's text carried on: 'Je ne mêlerai pas les genres', he declared: 'I will not mix genres'. Was this a simple observation, a statement of fact, or a vow, a promise sincerely made but not necessarily honoured? And when Derrida then repeated his own words, and said as much, asserting: 'I repeat: not to mix genres. I will not do so' (*P*, 233; *A*, 223; translation modified), was he merely repeating himself for emphasis or rather quoting himself, in which case might it not follow that the initial statement or injunction was itself already a silent quotation? Context was key, but in so far as the appeal to context by definition exceeded contextualisation, was the attribution of any phrase to one genre rather than another, one mode rather than another, or to a genre rather than a mode, or a mode rather than a genre, not full of possible pitfalls as inevitable as they were necessary?

The uncertainties of interpretation that Derrida highlights are not uncommon. In most situations speakers have little difficulty in deciding as to which of the forms or meanings available is the appropriate one. Derrida agrees. His paper, however, goes back a step to make two essential points. First, if a decision is necessary on the part of the listener or reader, it must be that there is more than one possible choice to be made. If so, then immediately prior to the decision being taken, there has to be a moment during which the available choices hang so to speak in mid-air, pending the decision to be taken, like so many virtual or phantom outcomes that are neither properly present nor properly absent. This moment of suspense or suspension may last barely an instant. It is however what makes decision both possible and necessary, and without it nothing would occur at all. So if a decision does occur, it can only be because something has already occurred, if only for the blink of an eye, to resist and defer that decision; and without that delay, not even present as present time, Derrida argues, whatever might be thought to happen would not be a decision, merely a pre-programmed, automatic response.

Decisions do get taken, then, obviously enough, but only in so far as they are fractured or divided by this absolutely irreducible blink of hesitation without which they would no longer be decisions. And whenever a decision is taken, even though it may have been taken, it always remains possible for the decision to have been otherwise. Though never present as such, Derrida argues, the trace of that possibility nevertheless survives as part of the memory of the decision, living on as a kind of spectral, ghostly trace, and a reminder of what might have been. Decisions are moreover not taken in the void, by lottery, or by machine. Time is needed: for consultation, deliberation, choice. And this was already Derrida's second point. It was that, when a decision is taken, in so far as it is a decision, it always implies some kind of rule or precept.

Derrida's argument can be readily confirmed by everyday experience. A neighbour, a friend, perhaps even a relative, male or female, is expecting a child. The child is born. Shortly after, you happen to meet the new parent(s) and baby, carefully wrapped up so as to be unrecognisable. What is the first question on your lips? What is it, you ask? Is it a boy or a girl? What did the stork bring? Both Derrida's points are neatly illustrated here. First, so long as the baby's sex is not made public (by word, gesture, or some other conventional sign, such as pink or blue clothing), it is only possible to refer to that child using an impersonal, neuter pronoun ('it'), even though, in virtually all other circumstances, when referring to a living person that pronoun would be judged inappropriate, even inhuman. What it signals here, however, is that, in so far as the child will be identified, in a moment, as *either* male *or* female, so, provisionally at least, for as long as identification is held in suspense, and as far as words are concerned, then she or he is *neither* female nor male, whence the neuter *it*.

In the vast majority of cases, the sexual identity of a human baby is determined speedily enough. But the possibility will always remain, as a virtual alternative, and perhaps an object of fantasy on the part of either the child or its parent(s), that he, she, I could always have been the sex I turned out *not* to be. For there to be merely one possible gender is a contradiction in terms. There is by definition always more than one gender. Any single gender always implies the existence of other genders. So in so far as you or I, by chromosomal lottery, find ourselves identified as belonging to this or that gender, then the fact of that identification, far from precluding the possibility of misidentification, actually invites or accentuates it, at the very least as a phantom alternative, which is why, whether we like it or not, as that which is most proper to us, each of us has a double, a secret sharer or shadowy twin, in the shape of the other we might have been, and in a sense always have the potential to become (as the possibility of gender reassignment makes clear). This is no doubt in part why gender identification for humans is the source of such fierce conflict, speculation, disturbance, or desire. This illustrates Derrida's second point. For gender identification in its turn is inseparable from a vast, shifting repertoire of cultural norms as enabling as they can be debilitating.

For whenever generic or gender-based decisions are made, the law is never far behind, decreeing, for instance, Derrida reminds us, that genres (and genders) are not to be mixed. But what if it were impossible, Derrida asks, *not* to mix them? If so, this would come as no surprise to the law prohibiting any such mixture, for a law that sought to repress what was not possible in the first place would hardly be of much use. It would be no law at all. If so, this meant the law against mixing genders and genres was already too late: genders and genres were already hopelessly, and necessarily, mixed. The law might attempt to impose its norms, its modes, its genres, and so on, but by doing so, paradoxically all it did was to reveal its fragility. The crime had already been committed, and the law, rather than preventing it, was little more than tacit acknowledgement that it was more likely unpreventable, in which case the law against mixing genres, far from being a founding principle, to be obeyed in all circumstances, had itself already been preceded by a counter-law, Derrida calls it, the law of the law of genre, which was a law of necessary heterogeneity or hybridity, 'a principle of contamination, a law of impurity, an economy of parasitic interference' (*P*, 237; *A*, 227; translation modified).

Derrida went on in the rest of his paper to draw out the implications of this irreducibly prior, incontrovertible, and always affirmative counter-law. He began by emphasising the rigorous impossibility of indisputable attribution to any single type, mode, or genre. The power of discrimination on which genre theory relied found itself thwarted from the outset. The consequences were damaging for any descriptive history of genres, and they were serious too for any attempt to appeal to the distinction between (formal, linguistic) modes and (literary, historical) genres, since here too it was likely to prove impossible to police that distinction without unacceptable violence on the one hand or damaging incoherence on the other. Also under threat, so to speak, was that great stalwart of literary history, and of all university courses organised around literary history: the representative example. For if it were no longer defensible, say, without massive inconsequentiality, to cite *Ulysses* or *To the Lighthouse*, as exemplary modernist texts, or *Gravity's Rainbow* or *If On A Winter's Night a Traveller* as typically postmodernist ones, then a whole busy sector of literary critical activity might find itself redundant.

Admittedly, the concerns Derrida raises are not unfamiliar to critics, teachers, or students, who know from experience how difficult it is to draw demarcation lines between literary genres, and how far individual works of literature resist categorisation. In this sense Derrida was not saying anything specialists did not already know. But what he did point out was that the empirical problems encountered in defining genres (and genders) were not simply the result of limited historical knowledge, conceptual shortcomings, or the potential mismatch between generic model and individual text, all of which might be overcome by further work in the archive, by more exact description of formal or historical constraints, or by more detailed understanding of texts and genres. The difficulties, Derrida argued, ran more deeply than this, for they had to do with the structure of generic attribution itself, which meant they were radically inescapable.

Derrida explains why this is so in the next section of his paper. Everything turns on a particular, insurmountable paradox. Derrida's demonstration is in three parts. First of all, he argues, any attribution of genre, in literature or elsewhere, can only occur on the basis of some minimal trait or characteristic that is generally acknowledged to be common to all members of a given corpus: western movies, science-fiction novels, Symbolist poetry, songs to be sung at funerals, and so on. Such genres can be identified either retrospectively or prospectively. One can extract from a given corpus of texts a list of shared characteristics that makes it possible to define that genre or sub-genre, and then make decisions about the admissibility or not of items that may be proposed for membership. Alternatively, one can hypothesise a generic corpus and search for items to allocate to it. Either way, it is a matter of constructing an inclusive set or class of objects and attributing items to it. Crucial here, as Derrida points out, is the logical hierarchy embodied in this tree-like structure. For just as a label is found only on the outside of a tin and not inside it, so the title, heading, or other descriptor that identifies, advertises, and regulates a genre cannot itself logically already be part of the genre it names (*P*, 243; *A*, 228–9). It may lay down the law about what may belong to a given genre, but it does so by standing on the threshold, as gate-keeper, allowing or refusing admission to this or that candidate on the basis of agreed criteria.

Derrida's second point has to do with the status of these minimal traits of belonging on the basis of which membership of a genre is awarded. It is, Derrida notes, part of the structure of any trait and any linguistic mark to allow itself to be re-marked, i.e. repeated, cited, referred to, folded back upon itself, detached from its context, or treated ironically, and so on (*P*, 243–4; *A*, 229). Derrida's own opening comments demonstrate this, and it is a condition that applies, too, to the mark of generic belonging. So it would always be possible, if unusual, for a gardening magazine, say, to draw its readers' attention to its membership of the genre of gardening magazines, and openly declare, so to speak: 'Look at me, I'm a gardening magazine' (*P*, 244; *A*, 229). This can always happen, even with the most modest of allotment society newsletters. But though one can never be sure, it would be unlikely to become a condition of membership of that genre.

In the case of literary or artistic genres, however, Derrida suggests, the situation is arguably rather different. For it is one of the few, perhaps even *only* property of a so-called work of art, he argues, that its belonging to a genre is *invariably* re-marked in one way or another by the work itself. 'What interests me', he writes, 'is that this re-mark, which is always possible with any text or corpus of traces, is absolutely necessary, and constitutive, in the case of what goes under the name of art, poetry, literature' (*P*, 244; *A*, 229; translation modified). If art has a defining characteristic, albeit more a minimal condition of possibility than a fully-fledged essence, he argues, then this is it. The claim, Derrida concedes, cannot be proven exhaustively, since to do so it would be necessary to list each and every one of the texts to which the clause may or may not apply, which simply cannot be done, for it would be impossible to know where to stop: it might indeed end up applying to everything, which would merely confirm that the limits of so-called literature are potentially unreachable.

In making this second move, Derrida was largely reiterating and generalising what he had argued apropos of Mallarmé ten years earlier, which is that words, in Mallarmé's prose and poems, and in principle everywhere else, in addition to meaning whatever it is they happen to mean, have the strange capacity to be folded back upon themselves according to the logic of the re-mark. It is possible, too, though it is nowhere explicit, that Derrida was reflecting, in his own way, on one of the most provocative and radical of artistic thought-experiments of the twentieth century, which was in the form of a found object, an industrially produced urinal, mockingly signed R. Mutt, dated 1917, and exhibited that same year under the title 'Fountain' at the Society of Independent Artists in New York by the painter and sculptor Marcel Duchamp. The piece was a sensation. It ironically mocked the institution and institutionalisation of art and its willingness to treat art objects with quasi-religious reverence. But by a further irony, Duchamp's sculpture was only able to achieve its polemical goal in so far as it declared itself *also* to be a piece of sculpture. And this was the question it asked: what 'is' sculpture? Its reply was the urinal itself, which said: there is no immortal essence of art, a work of art is an object that signs and names itself, and installs itself in a gallery or a museum – as a work of art.

Here was the paradox. Duchamp's 'Fountain' was a work of art in so far as it fulfilled the criteria for membership of that class of objects called works of art, and because, by the logic of the re-mark, it was able to present itself to its audience as such: 'Look', it said, with a perverse grin, 'I'm a sculpture, not a urinal.' By that very fact, however, according to the logic of generic attribution, there therefore had to be something in the presentation of the urinal that was not part of the genre called sculpture. In so far as the urinal declared itself to be a work of art, then, it could not wholly be that work of art. In a way this is not surprising; it was after all the urinal's ironic detachment or distance from its own presumed status as a work of art that allowed it to denounce the institution of art in the first place, as though it was not itself a work of art at all, but a merely functional object – like a urinal.

Derrida's argument, however, was not about the allegedly subversive status of so-called modernist works such as Duchamp's urinal; it had more to do with the condition of possibility of art and literature in general (*P*, 244; *A*, 230). Everything turned on the peculiar fact, deriving from the logic of the label discussed earlier, that all literary texts (not unlike humans, and for much the same reasons) were differentiated according to genre (or gender), but that the particular trait or characteristic that attributed a text (or person) to a given genre (or gender) was itself necessarily *not* part of that genre (or gender). 'The re-mark of belonging', Derrida put it, 'does not itself belong.' The observation, paradoxical though it is, was simple enough. Its implications, however, were vast. For what then followed, Derrida went on to argue, carefully distancing himself from any notion of Romantic creativity, was that

> no text can be thought to *belong* to a genre. Any text *participates* in one
> or more genres, there is no text without genre, genre and genres always
> exist, yet participation *in* a genre is never a belonging *to* a genre. This is
> not because of some overspill due to abundance or free, anarchic and
> unclassifiable productivity, but because of the *trait* of participation itself,
> the effect of code, and the mark of genre.
>
> (*P*, 245; *A*, 230; translation modified)

The clause of genre, Derrida notes, functions like a foreign body. It is neither
entirely assimilable nor entirely extraneous, and tends to be found in a place that
is neither properly inside nor properly outside the work. But by being stationed
on the threshold of the work, it serves simultaneously to demarcate and police
the boundaries of the genre *and* to interrupt that demarcation and those very
boundaries. The clause of genre, in other words, makes genres possible but also
makes them impossible; and there can be no such thing, therefore, as an single
pure genre (or gender).

Like all paradoxes, Derrida's point is both simple yet vertiginous, which is
why, as loyal speakers do, Derrida proceeded to offer his audience an example.
But this was to forget, up to a certain point, that the status of examples was
profoundly affected by Derrida's argument. For just as it is impossible *purely*
*and simply* to attribute a text to any one or more genre(s), so it is impossible
to cite an example that might *purely and simply* serve as an instantiation of
any given genre, which is to ask serious questions of genre theory, however
legitimate or useful it may be. By definition, then, any example was always
counter-exemplary (*P*, 266; *A*, 252), which did not mean simply that it might
contradict an accepted generic rule, or serve as an example of some alternative
generic convention, but, more radically, that it put into crisis the assumption
that examples were exemplary of anything other than themselves.

Any text was therefore singular. This did not mean it was some idealised,
unfathomable, transcendent creation to be admired from afar. What it did
mean was that, while every text participated in a genre, it was by that fact
irreducible to it. And if part of a text might be thought to be inside a given
genre, it was only because it was also simultaneously outside it. Where textuality
was concerned, it turned out not for the first time that the division between
an inside and an outside was impossible to maintain. By suggesting, famously,
that there was 'nothing outside of the text' Derrida had already said as much
about the relationship between text and context. There, too, there was mutual
implication, in that any text is inscribed within a specific, historically marked
context, but also an irreducibility of the one to the other, in that no given,
historical context can ever account exhaustively for the meaning or absence

of meaning of that text, which also meant that no context, any more than affiliation to genre or gender, was ever homogeneous.

Derrida turned his attention, then, to a singular text. The text he chose, as mentioned earlier, was a short, twenty-page first-person narrative, of the kind usually described in French as belonging to the genre of the *récit*, that had first appeared in 1949, but had more recently been republished under a changed title: Blanchot's *La Folie du jour* (*The Madness of the Day*). The story is a strange text to attempt to summarise, not least because what happens without happening in Blanchot's highly elliptical story is everything and nothing. The story's anonymous narrator begins by detailing a strangely wandering existence, in the course of which he repeatedly finds himself between states, places, even lives, and perpetually on the edge: 'Suffering numbs the mind', he tells the reader. 'But such', he adds, 'is the remarkable truth of which I am sure: I experience boundless pleasure in living and will find boundless satisfaction in dying.'[24] Halfway through the story, he has a brief, disconcerting vision: he glimpses a woman with a baby carriage trying to enter the courtyard of a building; a man arrives, half-enters, hesitates, then re-emerges, while the woman lifts up the pram, passes through, and disappears. 'This brief scene', comments the narrator, 'whipped me into a frenzy. I could barely explain it to myself no doubt, and yet I was sure, I had seized the moment after which the day, having stumbled upon a true event, was about to hurry towards its end. Here it comes, I said to myself, the end is coming; something is happening, the end is beginning.'[25] Shortly after, someone smashes glass in his eyes, almost blinding him, and he ends up in hospital. After a time, during which he has a series of conversations with a female figure personifying the law, he is asked by his two doctors, one of whom is an ophthalmologist and the other a psychiatrist, to give an account of himself. He refuses or is unable to satisfy their demands, and the story ends with the words: 'A story? No, no story, never again.'[26]

As Derrida's analysis of the relationship between text and genre suggested, everything here has to do with edges: beginnings, endings, frontiers, borders, margins. Derrida began his account of Blanchot's story, as he had Mallarmé's 'Mimique', by examining the space around the text, as occupied by the title, sub-title, and implicit generic descriptor, which, in the case of Blanchot's story, was a site of particular turbulence. Already in the essay 'Survivre', 'Living On', in *Deconstruction and Criticism*, Derrida had shown that the initial, 1949 title of Blanchot's story, first published in the journal *Empédocle*, had been somewhat different. According to the list of contents that appeared on the inside cover of the journal, as the heading of the actual story confirmed, it was called, simply enough: 'Un récit' ('A Story'); while on the front cover of the journal it was renamed with the addition of an oddly supplementary question mark: 'Un récit?' ('A Story?') (*P*, 122–6; *DC*, 87–9). This indecision on the part of the so-called original title – or titles – raised many questions. Was it an indication of genre, or did it identify the theme of the story? Was the title simply a quotation from the text, or a self-description? Was the presence or absence of the question mark to be taken ironically or not? And what guarantee was there that the title with the question mark, or the title without it, referred to the same work? And what was at stake in the replacement of both these original titles by the 1973 title, *La Folie du jour*, itself a quotation drawn from the twenty-first paragraph of this forty-one-paragraph-long story, that is, from the central articulation, the very fulcrum of Blanchot's narrative?

In 1973, when the story was republished, the word *récit*, narrative, which had originally served to present the story to its readers, had been displaced. It was no longer an uncertain title. But was it still an accurate generic description of the slim volume Blanchot had republished? This was the question Derrida went on to probe. From the outset, if Blanchot's story was a story, it was a story that, according to its narrator, narrated an inability to shape events into a story; and if it seemed, albeit with some hesitation or irony, to identify itself as a story, it did so only in order to withdraw from that identification. But this was not an isolated piece of textual trickery, Derrida argued, but for the reasons explored earlier a precise and sustained reflection on the paradoxical relationship between genre and text as such. As far as *La Folie du jour* was concerned, it resulted in the strangest of all literary topologies. Not without some wry humour, having earlier remarked on narratology's fondness for ever more outlandish terminological coinages, this was what Derrida called the 'double chiasmatic invagination of the edges' (*P*, 252; *A*, 238). The apparent barbarousness of the expression was, however, deceptive. In using the term invagination, a standard medical term for an internal organ folded inside out, deriving from the Latin *vagina*, meaning sheath or scabbard, Derrida was implicitly reminding his readers of that logic of the girdle explored via Freud's paper on 'Fetishism', according to which the relationship between inside and outside, rather than being fixed, was subject to an underlying reversibility, with the outside always able to pass inside and the inside pass outside, making it difficult in the end, if not impossible, to cling reliably to these indications of place as anything other than provisional sites of transition.

As with a glove turned inside out, so, then, with *La Folie du jour*. And when Derrida came to consider the edges or borders or framing of the text, notably its nominal beginning and ending, the structure he found was the following. Blanchot's story had opened with these words from its narrator: 'I am neither learned nor ignorant. I have known joys. That is an understatement: I am alive and being alive fills me with immense pleasure.' Some twenty pages later, shortly before the end of the story, asked by his doctors to tell them how 'exactly' things had happened, the narrator begins again: 'A story? I began: I am neither learned nor ignorant. I have known joys. That is an understatement. I told them the whole story, to which they listened, I think, with interest, at least at the beginning. But the end came as a surprise to us all. "When you've finished beginning," they said, "get to the facts." How come! The story was over.'[27]

As the beginning of the story is reprised in almost the exact same terms a page or so before its end, so the opening edge of the story is folded into the middle in such a way as to defeat any sense that here is a linear narrative hastening towards its end. If the reader takes the narrator's hint that the 'whole story' he recounts to the doctors is the whole story that the reader has just been reading, and which, by rights, should itself be quoted in its entirety by the narrator, so the business of telling the story becomes literally interminable. And what is also implied by the doctors' impatience for a proper story based on 'the facts', is that not only is the story interminable, it is hardly a story at all, rather an endless approach to something that only happens because it fails to happen, an approach to the ending that is paradoxically also a deferral of the ending.

There is a second fold in the story, too, Derrida writes, which cites or announces Blanchot's closing words ('A story? No, no story, never again') and brings them, so to speak, to the centre of the story in the form of the phrase: 'A story? I began . . .', cited above, albeit at a point that comes slightly earlier than where the previous fold joined the main body of the text, which means the story cannot simply be described as circular, since there is an impossible temporal or spatial overlap between the upper (beginning) edge and the lower (concluding) edge of the text. At this stage, Blanchot's decision to provide his 'original' text ('A Story' or 'A Story?') with a new title, taken from the centre of its own text, becomes easier to understand, for by bringing the centre to the edge it enacts a similar movement.

Blanchot's text is paradoxical, then, through and through. It is a text which properly neither begins nor ends but is perpetually beginning and ending, where nothing is a border but everything is, and where the centre is both everywhere and nowhere. It is both a story and not a story, a story with little narrative content, but which is nevertheless interminable, an approach to a story that is also a postponement of story, a movement of deferral that is infinite but also finite, indeed little more than twenty pages long. In so far as it refers throughout to its own status as a text that is and is not a story, it in that sense seems, somewhat bizarrely, to be capacious enough to include itself, like an inside pocket large enough to contain the overcoat into which it is fitted. Hierarchies are reversed and displaced, in a two-fold movement not very different from what Derrida describes elsewhere as the movement of deconstruction, and it is more impossible than ever, in dealing with Blanchot's story, and, by implication, with any other story, to distinguish between an outside and an inside, between that which may be said to imitate and that which may be said to be imitated.

But this is anything but a case of mere textual playfulness, or so-called postmodern or postpostmodern textual transgression. On the contrary, in its paradoxical relationship to story-telling, what Blanchot's story does is to display the conditions of possibility and impossibility of all story-telling. It does not break the law but exposes its folly. In any case, as Blanchot argues elsewhere, simply to subvert the law is at best a backhanded compliment, a gesture that, while claiming to defy the law, in the end submits to its authority.[28] In *La Folie du jour*, as the 1973 title reminds the reader, what is at stake is not the power or authority of the law, 'not the law with which everyone is familiar', says the narrator, 'which is severe and disagreeable',[29] but – its madness. By way of explanation Derrida takes the reader to that (almost) central scene – which, for the reasons we have been discussing, is neither the centre nor indeed a scene – in which the narrator describes being attacked: 'I almost lost my sight', he explains, 'someone having shattered glass in my eyes. The blow left me shaken, I must admit. It was like going straight into the wall, or straying into a thicket of flint. Worst of all was the sudden, awful cruelty of daylight; I could neither look nor prevent myself from looking; to see was terror itself, and to stop seeing a raking wound running from my forehead to my throat.' Shortly after, he adds: 'Eventually, I became convinced that what I was seeing, face to face, was the madness of the day; that was the truth: light was going mad, the brightness had lost all sense; it assailed me without reason, without rules, without purpose.'[30]

As Derrida points out, the simple word *jour* has a number of different meanings in French. As in English, it names that twenty-four hour period known as a day, but it can also refer, more broadly, to a given temporal event in particular, as well as to time in general. It can also mean: daylight, sunlight, the clear light of day; and in so far as it symbolises life, it often turns up in expressions such as: *donner le jour*, literally, to give daylight, meaning: to give birth. And like English daylight, it can also refer to the gap between things through which light is able to pass. All these associations, Derrida argues, are deeply implicated in Blanchot's story; but the one he opts to emphasise in 'The Law of Genre', for reasons of context, has to do with the logic of the gift. In that connection, the madness of the day relates principally to the question of the origin or the beginning, in a word, all that which, thanks to an inexplicable act of giving, is given in advance of anything else: before life, language, events, the rest. Not by chance, then, the connotations of the word *jour* in Blanchot's text are biblical, even apocalyptic in status. In the beginning, it may be recalled, 'God said, Let there be light: and there was light.' At which point, 'God called the light Day, and the darkness he called Night' (Gen. 1: 3–5).

But again there was paradox. As Blanchot's narrator discovers, daylight makes visible, but it also blinds. It gives clarity but also obscurity, reason but also madness. And the further paradox is that both are necessary, vision is only possible if, alongside light, there is also darkness. Pure light, like pure darkness, disables, and makes vision impossible. Blanchot's story, argues Derrida, is an attempt to account, inside narrative, outside narrative, in the very margins of all narrative, for the conjoined possibility *and* necessity of day *and* night, which is why Blanchot's narrator has no choice: to look or not to look. Vision is an opening – of world to eye, of eye to world – only in so far as it is simultaneously a closing – a darkening of the world that makes it visible to the eye, and the blinking motion of the eye that allows it to see the world. For good reason, therefore, Derrida uses the figure of the blink of the eye not only to describe the motif of vision in Blanchot's story, but also the opening and closing of the possibility of literary (and other) genres. In both cases what was crucial was that neither sight nor genre could be treated as modes of presence, only as flickering movements of difference and deferral, simultaneous opening and closing: *différance.*

What held for literary genre also applied to gender. There too paradox ruled. Not only did each gender entail the possibility of at least one or more others, it also implied something which, like the generic clause of inclusion, belonged in fact to neither gender, something that functioned as the marker of gender difference(s) and was, so to speak, gender difference(s) as such. This allowed Derrida in his account of *La Folie du jour* to extend the argument about the necessary heterogeneity or impurity of genres to sexual difference(s). It is not for nothing, Derrida suggests, that Blanchot's narrator, characterised grammatically as male, takes on various affirmative attributes he himself describes as feminine, nor is it by accident, though it is prompted by French idiom (since the law, *la loi*, in the language, as the law of language dictates, is always in the feminine), that this stereotypical image of male authority is recast in Blanchot's story as a gender-specific, sexually differentiated, seductive, but no less powerful female figure who is herself necessarily divided, impure, and heterogeneous, just like the narrator, her male companion who, standing apart from her, does not accompany her, which is not to say he is not also bound to her by dint of the heterogeneity and exteriority they share.

Gender in writing, Derrida argues, is a site of irreducible admixture. This explains his cautious and carefully nuanced relationship to the feminist literary and cultural theory increasingly prominent from the 1970s onwards, and to which Derrida's Strasbourg paper, especially in so far as the question of the gift was concerned, was in part an oblique response (*A*, 58–9; *PS*, 95–115; 89–108). From the outset, as the thought of *différance* demanded, Derrida consistently opposed any neutralisation of difference in general, including sexual differences (Derrida insisted on the plural), which was a standard feature of metaphysical discourse. But this did not equate to a desire to thematise sexual differences in any stable, standard, or static way. The counter-law of impurity and heterogeneity affirmed in and by *La Folie du jour* made it impossible for Derrida in any rigorous way to subordinate sexual differences to any sex- or gender-based identity, and in the end (though it might in given circumstances have some limited tactical justification) made any theory of literature that posited such identity on the part of writers or readers philosophically unsustainable.

## A purloined letter

In the France of the 1960s and 1970s one of the most influential yet fiercely debated bodies of thought available to literary critics and theorists was Freudian psychoanalysis. It had not always been so. In the early decades of the century, notwithstanding the enthusiasm of such writers and artists as the Surrealist André Breton, France had been relatively resistant to psychoanalysis, which it viewed with suspicion as representing something essentially alien to the French Cartesian mind. But matters began to change after the Second World War, not least because of the interest in Freud's work shown by post-war French philosophy.

This did not however make psychoanalysis any less controversial. And at the centre of most, if not all the heated confrontations that were to mark psychoanalysis in France over the next thirty years and show no sign of abating even today, was the powerful, pioneering, yet idiosyncratic figure of Jacques Lacan (1901–81). From the early 1950s onwards, in a series of notorious weekly seminars primarily addressed to fellow analysts, and in various stylistically challenging, philosophically informed, and often provocative theoretical papers collected in 1966 under the title *Ecrits* (*Writings*), Lacan had advanced the case for what he presented as a return to Freud, a return, he argued, that would reverse the conformist, normalising tendencies of much post-Freudian, notably American analysis.

This was a return, then, with a difference. For the Freud Lacan thought it essential to rescue from distortion was not the Freud who had looked to the natural sciences for inspiration in exploring the unconscious, but the Freud who in such trail-blazing works as *The Interpretation of Dreams* (1900), *The*

*Psychopathology of Everyday Life* (1901), and *Jokes and their Relation to the Unconscious* (1905) had put forward a radical new understanding of language and meaning. After Copernicus, after Darwin, Freud was the third great revolutionary of modern times, who was best understood, Lacan argued, as an almost exact contemporary of Saussure, who, had the opportunity been available, would have framed the theory of the unconscious in less biologistic, explicitly linguistic terms.

It was Lacan's task, as he saw it, to uncover and develop further this hitherto obscured dimension of Freud's thought. For just as a dream is accessible to interpretation only as a remembered, half-forgotten text, and just as a physical or psychological symptom may be understood only if, like the dream, it is regarded as having been written in a kind of code, spoken in an unknown language belonging only to the patient or analysand, so the unconscious, Lacan contended, appealing as he did so to the work of Saussure, Jakobson, and Lévi-Strauss, 'was structured like a language [*comme un langage*]'. This was not to say that the unconscious was reducible as such to any given natural language (*la langue*), but that it was structured in a similar way to language(s) in general, and that it was therefore possible to analyse the logic of the unconscious, what Lacan went on to call the Symbolic, with the aid of the Saussurean theory of the sign, that is, by deploying the concepts of signifier and signified.

There was however a necessary displacement. For while according to standard Saussurean theory signifier and signified were like the two sides of a single sheet of paper, and the relationship between them arbitrary or unmotivated, this did not entirely hold for the unconscious. Just as Freud had suggested in *The Interpretation of Dreams* that in a dream any discrete element of sense, by condensation or displacement, might come to stand in for any number of apparently unrelated motifs, echoing down the never-ending chains of unconscious association on the basis of phonetic or graphic similarities between words, so in the unconscious, Lacan argued, the signifier became split from its signified, which, as far as the manifest content of the dream was concerned, was present only in travestied, displaced, and repressed form, accessible, if at all, only at the end of a lengthy, in principle interminable process of analysis. What constituted the human subject, then, was not the sign, but the logic of the autonomous, unconscious signifier; and alongside Freud, in order to articulate that logic, Lacan drew on many other, explicitly philosophical sources, most notably the post-Hegelian thinking of Alexandre Kojève, whose weekly seminar on Hegel's *Phenomenology of Spirit* Lacan had attended between 1933 and 1939, together with such other key figures of the period as the novelist, essayist, and cultural critic Georges Bataille, Sartre's friend the philosopher Raymond Aron, the novelist Raymond Queneau, and the essayist, translator, and future novelist and painter Pierre Klossowski. Lacan, however, did not stop there. In later years, he exploited modern mathematics, set theory, and topology in similar ways, too, as part of an effort to arrive at a rigorous formalisation of the logic of the unconscious, though some would insist its status was at best merely metaphorical.

In some ways, Lacan's approach was not entirely new. Psychoanalysis in general had long displayed an interest not only in the workings of language, but also in literary and other works of the imagination. Some of Freud's most famous propositions, including that cornerstone of his thinking about human sexuality and desire, the theory of the Oedipus complex, had their origins in art, literature, or myth, to which Freud would often return, as he did to Shakespeare, E. T. A. Hoffmann, Leonardo, Michelangelo, or the Greeks, in search of elucidation or confirmation of what he was beginning to unearth in his clinical work.

At an earlier stage in his career, Lacan, too, had been far more receptive than most to developments in art and poetry, and was briefly associated, in the early 1930s, with elements in the French Surrealist movement. Literary texts and other works of various kinds were also often cited in his weekly seminars. And in 1966, when he brought together his most important theoretical papers in an otherwise broadly chronological 900-page volume, Lacan foregrounded the central role of literature for psychoanalysis by opening the volume with a presentation based on an interpretation of a well-known short story, made famous in France because of the deep personal interest shown in its author by the poet Charles Baudelaire, who also translated it, and by Mallarmé, another influential admirer and translator of his poems. The story was called 'The Purloined Letter'; its author was the American writer Edgar Allan Poe.

This was not the first time psychoanalysis had been drawn to Poe's fantasmatically compelling work. The Gothic or Romantic tale hovering midway between reality and fantasy had been a favourite object of inquiry for Freud, who had written on Jensen's 'Gradiva' in 1907 and Hoffmann's 'Sandman' in 1919; and following Freud's lead in 1933, Marie Bonaparte (1882–1962), one of the co-founders of the inaugural Société psychanalytique de Paris (Paris Psychoanalytic Society), and regarded by many at the time as Freud's unofficial representative in France, published an orthodox, biographically based psychoanalytic study of Poe's work, prefaced by Freud himself, who paid homage to the book's author by declaring that '[t]hanks to her interpretative effort, we now realise how many of the characteristics of Poe's work were conditioned by his personality, and can see how that personality derived from intense emotional fixations and painful infantile experiences'.[31] In later years, following a series of events that culminated in 1953 in a dramatic scission at the heart of the SPP, resulting in the departure of Lacan and several colleagues to set up the rival Société française de psychanalyse (French Society of Psychoanalysis), Bonaparte and Lacan were to become bitter enemies in their competing claims to Freud's intellectual and institutional legacy. The struggle was an uncompromising one on both sides, and forms at least some of the hidden subtext of Lacan's reading of Poe's story, which he first presented to his seminar in April 1955, wrote up the following year, and finally published in 1957.[32]

'The Purloined Letter', completed by Poe in 1844, has its place in history mainly as an influential precursor of the modern detective story. Its plot turned on a paradox which, as the story itself suggests, was simple and obvious, yet odd and enigmatic. One evening, the detective Auguste Dupin and his unnamed male companion who narrates the story are sitting in darkness in Dupin's smoke-filled back-library, or book-closet, as Poe calls it, in the faubourg Saint-Germain in Paris, when they are interrupted by a visit from the local Prefect of Police, who has a pressing dilemma. An unscrupulous minister in the government, known only as D—, during an interview with the Queen and in full view of the King (thus explaining the Queen's inability to act), has stolen from her a (sexually?) compromising letter, putting a substitute missive of his own in its place. The Queen knows the thief's identity, but this only increases the minister's power over her, albeit with the corollary, observes the narrator, that his hold over the Queen would come to nothing if he were to release the letter (underlining the extent to which what counts here, as Lacan will argue, is the power or potency of the letter, far more than the prestige or social standing of whoever believes they have it in their possession). So far, in the attempt to retrieve the missing letter, the Prefect explains, he and his men have subjected the minister's apartments to ever more rigorous physical scrutiny, but to no avail. The letter remains enigmatically hidden.

A month later, however, the Prefect makes a return visit to Dupin and his companion, at the end of which, in exchange for 50,000 francs, Dupin triumphantly produces the incriminating letter and hands it to the astonished Prefect who promptly leaves. Dupin now goes on to explain to the narrator how he gained possession of the letter. Between the Prefect's two visits, he reports, he had called to see the minister, armed with a pair of green spectacles, and had spotted the letter in D—'s apartment, where it lay truly hidden only because it was in the most obvious place possible, sitting openly displayed in 'a trumpery filigree card-rack of pasteboard, that hung dangling by a dirty blue ribbon, from a little brass knob just beneath the middle of the mantelpiece'. In the rack was thrust a solitary letter, 'much soiled and crumpled', and 'torn nearly in two, across the middle – as if a design, in the first instance, to tear it up entirely as worthless, had been altered, or stayed, in the second'.[33] Under the

pretext of having forgotten his snuff-box, Dupin makes another visit to D—
the following day, and thanks to a carefully planned diversion that distracts
his adversary's attention, substitutes a letter of his own for the letter purloined
from the Queen, which he is thus able to sell back to the Prefect.

Here, then, is a story built around a complex series of repetitions and
duplications: two characters, Dupin and the narrator, sitting in a darkened
library; two visits to them by the Prefect; two scenes, one related by the Prefect,
the other by Dupin, in which a secret letter is spotted in full view of all, and
appropriated by another in the presence of the current (temporary) owner; two
visits by the detective Dupin to the villain D— ; and two scheming individuals, each endowed with superior analytical *and* imaginative powers, the one
a detective, the other a poet and mathematician, and who, sharing the same
initial letter, are the double and rival of the other and may even be brothers;
and so on. Lacan's interpretative strategy is not, however, to linger on these odd
but almost too self-evident textual doublings; it is to peer beneath the surface
of the story with something akin to green spectacles in order to plot the logic
driving the circular movement of the letter, taking the word here not only to
mean a missive or epistolary communication (as it does in Poe's story), but as
a synonym for the Saussurean or, better, Lacanian signifier. Lacan's purpose
in this was primarily didactic: it was to use 'The Purloined Letter' not only as
a text that might be read psychoanalytically, as Bonaparte had done (and had
been criticised for doing in too biographically reductive a fashion), but also,
and more powerfully, as an illustration of what Lacan presented as the truth
of Freudian thinking, according to which, in the analyst's own words, 'it is the
symbolic order [i.e. the logic of the unconscious signifier] that, as far as the
subject is concerned, is constitutive [i.e. it is both what makes the subject what
it is, and is the single most important factor in determining the subject's own
experience]'.[34]

The main focus of the 1954–5 seminar series in which Lacan first presented
his reading of 'The Purloined Letter' was that 'compulsion to repeat' or *Wieder-
holungszwang* that had posed Freud such theoretical difficulties in the period
following the First World War, and which he was to resolve only by famously
positing, in *Beyond the Pleasure Principle* (1920), the existence of an entropic,
disaggregating force in the unconscious which he called the 'death drive'. This
late turn in Freudian theory was immediately a subject of debate among psychoanalysts, many of whom remained sceptical as to its necessity. Not so Lacan,
however, who discovered in the Freudian death drive proof of his own fidelity
to Freud's legacy, for the simple reason, as he put it, quoting Saint Paul, that
'the letter killeth, but the spirit giveth life' (2 Corinthians 3: 6). What was true
of the death drive, in other words, was true of the signifier, and vice versa.

In 'The Purloined Letter', as far as Lacan was concerned, everything hinged, then, on repetition. And repetition in the story, he claimed, unfolded according to a threefold structure comprising three temporal moments, three looks or gazes, and three subject positions, occupied at different points in the text by one or more characters. 'The first', says Lacan, 'relates to a look that sees nothing: the King, and the police. The second relates to a look that sees the first sees nothing and deludes itself into believing that what it conceals is covered by it: the Queen, then the minister'; while 'the third sees that these first two looks leave exposed what should be hidden, ready to be seized by whoever dares: the Minister, and finally Dupin.'[35] As the letter circulates through the story, from initial ducal admirer to Queen to minister to Dupin to Prefect and finally, perhaps, the Queen again, it deals out to each of the characters in the text, according to Lacan, one or other of a series of roles corresponding to so many positions of unconscious sexual desire. 'If there is any meaning', Lacan concludes, 'in what Freud discovered and carried on rediscovering with an ever greater sense of peering over the precipice, it is that the displacement of the signifier determines subjects in their acts and destiny, their refusals and moments of blindness, their success and ultimate lot, notwithstanding their innate gifts and social standing, and irrespective of character or sex, and that, willy-nilly, everything which is part of individual psychology, having entirely capitulated to it, follows in the signifier's wake.'[36]

If the letter as it circulates through the story distributes male and female positions (which do not necessarily coincide with biological or anatomical gender) to those caught up in Poe's plot in this way, it is because the letter or signifier for Lacan is a marker – *the* marker – of sexual difference. For Lacan, closely following Freud, this reduces to a function of the presence or absence of what he terms the phallus: less an inflated version of the male penis than a symbol of its possible presence or absence, and therefore of the difference between male and female sexes. But the phallus is also more than this. For Lacan, in so far as it always presupposes the threat of castration and thus provides a privileged example of something present referring to something absent, the phallus also signifies the signifier itself, for the signifier too, following Saussure, may also be described as something present, i.e., a phonetic or graphic representation standing in for the necessarily absent object to which it refers. All of which means that the phallus, for Lacan, does not have the status of one mere signifier among others (as some feminists sympathetic to Lacan have been willing to believe), but that of a master signifier, which acts as the signified of all other signifiers, and by dint of its simultaneous presence–absence sums up not only the difference between the sexes, but the essence of all desire, which for Lacan, as it was for the post-Hegelian Kojève, is grounded on lack, i.e., on the tortuous circumstance that I only desire what I do not and cannot possess.

For Lacan the significance of the phallus does not stop here. For in so far as it is the crucial linchpin in what Lacan calls the Symbolic, the phallus also marks the difference between the human order of the signifier and the deliriously a-signifying world of psychosis deemed to stand beyond the cultural or linguistic pale of humanity itself.[37] And from this privileged status of the phallus as the letter or signifier of all desire flow two further principles crucial for Lacan's interpretation: firstly, that, however much it may be tattered or torn, substituted or stolen, turned inside out or replaced, like the missive in Poe's story, the signifier always remains the same, one and indivisible; and, secondly, that, as the letter migrates from one position to another, the trajectory it follows is always proper to it, marked out in advance, in that what is at stake in the movement of the signifier is what Lacan himself terms: destiny – which may not coincide with anatomy but is nevertheless binding.

In 'The Purloined Letter', then, according to Lacan, the missive always ends up where it began, with the Queen, the Mother, and with an unspeakable Oedipal desire for the Mother, and perhaps the Father, too. So it came as no surprise to Lacan (any more than it had to Bonaparte) that Dupin, in the role of surrogate psychoanalyst, his green spectacles standing in for the 'evenly suspended attention' recommended by Freud, should find the letter in a makeshift card-rack hanging down from a diminutive clitoridal brass knob over an empty, castrated, cloacal hearth, an incriminating reminder of the mother's absent penis. ('Other tales by Poe', observed Bonaparte, as she concluded her discussion of 'The Black Cat', 'also express, though in different and less aggressive fashion, regret for the missing maternal penis, with reproach for its loss. First among these, strange though it may seem, is "The Purloined Letter".'[38])

But it is time to bring this detour to an end, and return to Derrida, whose own engagement with Freud's legacy was complex and protracted. An early indication of this attention to the philosophical and more-than-philosophical implications of Freudian theory on Derrida's part came in a lecture entitled 'Freud and the Scene of Writing' delivered to an audience of psychoanalysts in March 1966 and published the following year in *Writing and Difference* (*WD*, 293–340; 246–91). The burden of the lecture was two-fold. On the one hand, Derrida argued, Freudian theory could not *not* be a part of that vast territory known as Western metaphysics, on which psychoanalysis had been obliged to draw in order to elaborate its own conceptual tools, from which it therefore followed, Derrida put it, that 'all Freudian concepts, without a single exception, belong to the history of metaphysics, that is, to that system of logo-centric repression which took shape as a way of excluding or demeaning the body of the written trace, thereby putting it out or putting it down, and treating it as a mere didactic, technical metaphor or like servile matter or excrement' (*WD*, 294; 247–8; translation modified). At the same time or, rather, not at the same time, precisely because Freud's exploration of the unconscious allowed him to envisage a strange kind of deferred temporality by which early memo-ries acquired their meaning(s) only after the event, when reactivated by later experience, without either the early memory or the later experience ever being properly present to consciousness, there was something in Freud, a thought of non-presence, original supplementarity, and textual excess, 'doubtless the only one', Derrida remarked, 'not to exhaust itself within metaphysics or science' (*WD*, 314; 266; translation modified), which might be considered to have begun to move beyond the conceptual horizon of metaphysics.[39] Language, too, from the perspective of Freud's work looked very different: no longer a transpar-ent medium for speech, more a layered hieroglyphic cipher, irreducible to the purity or transparency of intention, functioning more like a trace in memory the very possibility of which confirmed the thought of *différance*.

The relationship between Freud and Derrida was anything but one-sided. If it was true, on the one hand, Derrida sometimes remarked, that deconstruction would not have been possible without Freudian psychoanalysis, this did not mean it was in any sense reducible to it. It was rather that deconstruction had a vital contribution to make in scrutinising the philosophical assumptions that remained embedded in psychoanalytic theory, in dismantling, renewing, and radicalising them.

Derrida's interest in Freud did not therefore end in 1966. In the decades that followed, there were few more sustained or, on occasion, more fraught dialogues than that taking place (or sometimes not taking place) between Derrida and psychoanalysis. Numerous books, seminars, lectures, and papers, from *Glas* (1974; translated 1986) and *La Carte postale* (1980; *The Post Card*, 1987) to *Psyché: inventions de l'autre* (1987), *Mal d'archive* (1995; *Archive Fever*, 1996), *Résistances de la psychanalyse* (1996; *Resistances of Psychoanalysis*, 1998), or *États d'âme de la psychanalyse* (2000; *Without Alibi*, 2002), to mention only the most prominent, all bear witness to Derrida's continuing engagement not only with Freud's own writing and psychoanalytical theory in general, but also with the complex institutional, at times bitterly factional, and political issues that were inseparable from Freud's legacy. Perhaps not surprisingly, what lay at the centre of Derrida's dialogue with analysis and with certain analysts, notably his friends Nicolas Abraham and Maria Torok (whose study of cryptic language in Freud's Wolf Man case Derrida prefaced at length in 1976),[40] was precisely the question of inheritance: of writing, memory, the archive, responsibility for others and the other.

Though its explicit occasion was delayed until the early to mid-1970s, it was inevitable therefore that, in developing his own work in response and in relation to psychoanalysis, Derrida would at some stage have to address the work of the pre-eminent philosophically informed analyst of his generation, none other than Lacan himself. In 1990, a decade after the latter's death, at a conference on his relationship with philosophy (and philosophers), held at a time of deep conservative retrenchment in France, Derrida expressed his own powerful sentiment as follows: 'Whether one is dealing with philosophy, psychoanalysis, or theory in general', he declared, 'what the current climate of conformist restoration is busily trying to conceal, deny, or prevent us from saying, is that nothing of what helped transform the space of thinking in recent decades would have been possible without settling an argument *with* Lacan, and without Lacan's own provocative input, whatever one thinks or says about it, and, I would add, without settling an argument *with* Lacan's own settling of arguments *with* philosophers' (*R*, 64; 46; translation modified).

It was in 1975, in an essay later incorporated into *The Post Card*, having indicated the main thrust of his reading in a long footnote to an interview first published in 1971 (*Po*, 112–19; 107–13), that Derrida began settling at least part of the argument with Lacan as it touched on the relationship between psychoanalysis and literature. The site of the encounter, obviously enough, was Lacan's Seminar on 'The Purloined Letter' which Derrida examined in close detail. The title he gave his essay was 'Le Facteur de la vérité', which Alan Bass, translating Derrida's book, opts to leave in French. It might however be rendered: 'The Truth Factor', so long as the word is taken to mean not only an agent or element in a calculation, but also – a postman. For this was Derrida's theme or, better, heterogeneous non-theme (in much the same way that the book's reading of *Beyond the Pleasure Principle* was concerned not with 'la thèse' or the thesis presented in Freud's paper, but 'l'athèse' or a-thesis deployed or, more accurately, deferred in it (*PC*, 277–91; 259–73)): the question of positing, positioning, and posting in general, and of the various sorts of positions, posts, and postings this entailed, not to mention the numerous other kinds of posties, postilions, and postiches inseparable from it.

Derrida began, then, by inquiring into the relative positions, posts, or places occupied in turn by the thing called literature and that called psychoanalysis. As elsewhere, his opening words were pointedly pregnant. 'La psychanalyse, à supposer, se trouve' (*PC*, 441; 413), wrote Derrida, exploiting the double meanings enabled by the Latinate legacy of French grammar to advance at least four distinct propositions: first, that, yes, it may be supposed that psychoanalysis can be found somewhere, and that something called psychoanalysis indeed exists or happens; second, that psychoanalysis, supposedly, according to its originator(s) and proponents, found or discovered itself in an act of bold, spontaneous intellectual creation, and continues to be refound, again and again, whenever in the consulting room analyst encounters analysand; third, that psychoanalysis was capable of finding itself, determining its own place, circumscribing its territory and frontiers, saying what it was and was not; and, fourth, that psychoanalysis found or discovered itself by making suppositions, that is, by advancing hypotheses that were held to be true, by placing under itself (from the Latin: *sub-ponere, sub-position, sup-position*) theoretical claims whose function was to establish the truth of psychoanalysis, either in the sense that psychoanalysis corresponded to an objective state of affairs, as Freud contended, or in the sense that it brought forth a truth of its own, the truth of unconscious desire, as Lacan, having read and translated some Heidegger, preferred to put it.

For Derrida, not for the first or last time, everything turned on the possibility of rigorously separating inside from outside, of drawing and policing an authoritative line of demarcation between psychoanalysis and its others, its rivals or relatives. From quite early on in the history of psychoanalysis, it had become apparent that its boundaries were anything but impermeable, as Freud cheerfully conceded on a number of occasions, most famously perhaps in 1911 when he concluded one of his best documented case histories, dealing with the paranoid imaginings of the Dresden judge Dr Daniel Paul Schreber as recounted in his autobiography, by observing ruefully that 'it remains for the future to decide whether there is more delusion in my theory than I should like to admit, or whether there is more truth in Schreber's delusions than others are as yet prepared to believe'.[41] And it was not only the opposition between psychoanalytic theory and speculative madness that was unstable; the division between psychoanalysis and literature was intensely fragile too.

Not for nothing, therefore, in *The Interpretation of Dreams* was Freud ready to compare the gradual revelation of the terrible truth of parricide and incest in Sophocles' *Oedipus Rex* with the work of interpretation and reconstruction carried out in the psychoanalytic session.[42] Nor was it by chance that, two pages later, pursuing his discussion of the Oedipus complex at the heart of both Sophocles' play and Shakespeare's *Hamlet*, Freud was willing to enlist the support of a literary example to illustrate the distinction between primary unconscious material and secondary elaboration (what might be described in less technical terms as its original dream content and subsequent formal reworking). The example used was Hans Christian Andersen's famous story, 'The Emperor's New Clothes', in which, Freud wrote, using the story in part as a model for the unconscious, 'the impostor is the dream and the Emperor the dreamer himself, while the moralising tendency [in the story] reveals an obscure awareness of the fact that the latent dream content is concerned with forbidden wishes that have fallen victim to repression'.[43] Freud's choice of text, though, as Derrida points out, was far from indifferent: on either side, in literary example and psychoanalytical protocol, what was at issue was the desire to grasp the naked truth, as embodied in the truth of nakedness (*PC*, 444–8; 416–19). It was arguably less a case of psychoanalysis explaining literature than of literature rehearsing psychoanalysis; and less a case of literature illustrating psychoanalysis than of psychoanalysis repeating literature.

So it was not only that literature already inhabited psychoanalysis, in a figure such as Oedipus, say; it was that psychoanalysis itself already inhabited literature, in this case in the shape of a story about deception, disguise, nudity, and truth. Mallarmé's 'Mimique' and Blanchot's *La Folie du jour* had already testified to the difficulty of determining or policing boundaries. In Freud too, inside was also outside and outside was also inside, with literature and psychoanalysis alike both belonging to the same infinite general text (which, in Derrida, extended far beyond language or words in the strict or limited sense). The hierarchical superiority over the object of literature that psychoanalytic theory after Freud sought to claim was arguably precarious in the extreme, and the borders between the one and the other were increasingly hard, if not impossible, to maintain.

In these circumstances, Derrida now asked, what was the status of a work of fiction that not only claimed to reveal the truth, and said so at some length, and of which it was claimed by psychoanalytic theory that it delivered not only the truth of the matter but the truth of sexual desire in general? What was the status, in other words, of a literary text of which it was said that it already displayed the truth of desire, which it then fell to theory to repeat, glossing the truth the story had presented by deploying a second discourse on truth, a discourse on the truth of the truth? If Poe's Dupin was already an analyst *avant la lettre* (purloined or not), already spelling out the rudiments of Lacanian theory, did this not imply that Lacan the psychoanalytic interpreter had no option but to double up in turn as a latter-day Paris detective investigating the missing letter?

This, for Derrida, was exactly the position in the Seminar on 'The Purloined Letter'. It prompted him to ask as follows:

> For example: what happens in the psychoanalytical deciphering of a text when the text, i.e. that which is being deciphered, itself already explains itself? When it knows more about what is to be known than the one doing the deciphering (a debt acknowledged by Freud on more than one

occasion)? And especially when it, *moreover* [*de surcroît*: i.e. in addition, into the bargain, on top of everything else, as an always extra, supplementary trait; author's emphasis], includes within itself the scene of decipherment? When it deploys more force in staging and setting the analytic process adrift, up to and including the very last word, like truth, for example?

Derrida went on:

> The truth, for example. But is truth an example? What happens – and what is left out – when a text, for example a so-called literary fiction – but is this still an example? – stages the truth, and, in so doing, circumscribes [*délimite*: i.e. by staging it, in effect draws a line around it, marks its boundaries, and points silently beyond it] the psychoanalytic reading, assigns a position to the analyst, shows him searching for truth, finding it even, holding forth on the truth of the text, and then articulating in general the discourse on truth, and on the truth of truth? What is it that does without a text capable of such a scene, fully confident in its capacity to put in their place all of psychoanalysis's comings and goings in its dealings with truth?    (*PC*, 442; 414; translation modified)

The answer could only be that truth, far from commanding the story from the outset, as Lacan contended, in fact came second, was more a product or effect of the writing which made it possible and which, as it lifted the curtain onto the stage where truth or untruth might appear, was itself necessarily *neither* true *nor* untrue, but, in so far as it preceded both, more powerful than either. This did not commit Derrida to the self-defeating claim, sometimes associated with the urban myth of 'fictive deconstructionism',[44] that truth itself was a fiction, from which it might then follow that rational argument was mere sophistry. Nothing could be further from what Derrida actually wrote. For Derrida, it was more a matter of paying ever more rigorous, scrupulous attention to the conditions of possibility and the emergence of truth. What was required therefore, against all dogmatism, and in the name of truth, was an ever greater awareness of the complexity of truth claims in general. More particularly, on Derrida's part, as far as so-called literary texts are concerned, it was imperative not to treat literature as the expression of established, institutionalised truth or truths, not least because such an assumption or expectation could not *not* culminate in conformist dogma, the effect of which was to efface the singular futurity of writing as an event intervening affirmatively into the world precisely in order to challenge the closed horizon of supposed presence and identity.

Derrida recognised of course that Lacan's psychoanalytic reading of Poe was very different from the largely biographical interpretation offered by Bonaparte.

Not for Lacan the tale of mystery and imagination that was the story of Poe's parents, the sudden departure and probable death of his biological father at the age of one, the untimely early demise of his 'ethereal and wan' actress mother at the age of two, his grudging adoption by his foster father John Allan, all of which ended, according to Bonaparte, as she endeavoured to prove on the basis of the author's texts, in the writer's obsessive fixation on the figure of the 'live-in-death mother' and his rebellious assault on his luckless stand-in father.

By largely excluding all of this, and by reframing his interpretation of 'The Purloined Letter' in such a way as to focus attention solely on the circulation of the letter as signifier of desire, Lacan, Derrida conceded, brought a new and legitimate formal sophistication to the dialogue between psychoanalysis and literature. But Lacan's new psychoanalytic order was not without difficulties of its own; and Derrida goes so far as to suggest (the argument is developed further in *Glas*), that its formalism was at best the obverse of the psychological thematicism it sought to replace. For what both the privileging of themes and the prioritising of the formal properties of a text had in common was their confident belief in the stability of their framing of the text, which, here as there, in different but symmetrical fashion, served to position the text as present to itself as meaning or as form. 'Formalism and hermeneutic semanticism', remarked Derrida, 'are always at one: the difference between them is just a matter of where you put the frame' (*PC*, 460; 432; translation modified).

Throughout the early part of the 1970s, most explicitly in a 1974 essay on Kant's *Critique of Judgement*, entitled 'Parergon' (the word, from the Greek, means an ornamental accessory, a subsidiary or supplementary work, and figures importantly in Kant when the philosopher is considering, again on the basis of examples, what is essential to the artwork and what is secondary to it (*TP*, 62–6; 53–6)), Derrida explored in some detail the precarious double or dual status of frames. Like titles, and like attributions of genre, which are themselves already frames of a sort, frames in general are by definition always divided. The frame belongs to the work, which it announces or presents as such to its readers or viewers; but equally it stands at a distance from the work, which is how and why it can point to the work, and provide it with a name, a title, and an identity. A frame, at one and the same time, both detaches a work from its context and re-attaches to that context. (Language students for instance, in a translation or reading exercise, will often acknowledge the divided character of the frame by asking whether they should translate or read its title. Is the title an integral part of the text, they ask, or an extraneous label to be set aside? Similarly, if one is copying or forging a painting, is it necessary, or not, also to copy or forge the frame?)

This logic of the frame was nothing new. Under another name, it was exactly the same, and for the same reasons, as the double logic governing, among others, the supplement (in *Of Grammatology*), context (in 'Signature Event Context'), and genre (in 'The Law of Genre'). Like these others, frames too are unavoidable, since an absence of frame is itself already a frame, but no frame ever permanently closes off what it surrounds. The fact that a frame (or absence of frame) is always possible also means that supplementary or additional frames, which do not need to be visible, can keep on being added to the first, opening the artwork up, again and again, in a movement of constant repetition that is in principle endless. Each frame, then, is also a fracture, an articulation that joins as it disjoins, and vice versa. But as with the infinite number of possible contexts to which a given text may be transferred, or onto which it may be grafted, this proliferation of potential frames should not cause dismay on the part of would-be interpreters. Without the constant possibility of framing and reframing, the meaning of any text would be absolutely fixed, once and for all, and it would no longer be possible to interpret, to read, or study anything. And this goes not only for literary criticism; it applies even more insistently to the possibility of psychoanalysis itself.

In this respect what is most revealing about Lacan's interpretation of 'The Purloined Letter' was what Lacan chose to exclude, which for the most part had to do with the framing effects at work in Poe's story. First of all, as Derrida shows, Lacan reduces the three scenes (at least) in Poe's narrative (the story of the Prefect's visit to Dupin and the narrator; the story of the Prefect's second visit to the pair, a month later; the story of the double visit by Dupin to the Minister D— ) to two triangular plot events, i.e. D— 's appropriation of the Queen's letter in the presence of the King, which Lacan situates or positions as the story's 'primal scene', using the term coined by Freud to describe that first traumatic moment when, in reality or fantasy, the child witnesses parental intercourse, then followed by Dupin's reappropriation of the letter from D— , facilitated by a convenient disturbance in the street (*PC*, 456; 429).[45] In Lacan's expeditious retelling of Poe's story for didactic purposes, what then is left out, or neutralised, as Derrida more accurately puts it, is the part played and the commentary offered by the first-person narrator through whom everything in the text, from beginning to end, is mediated, as the numerous quotation or speech marks scattered throughout Poe's story indicate (*PC*, 459; 431). (Here, as elsewhere, Derrida's project, it could be said, is to measure the incalculable implications of the fact that any mark can always be re-marked, surrounded for instance by quotation marks and divorced from its present context, to which it cannot therefore be said wholly or entirely ever to belong; any mark, in other words, is always already transferential.)

Much like Dr Watson in Conan Doyle's Sherlock Holmes stories, whom he largely models, Poe's narrator doubles up in 'The Purloined Letter' as both the source of the narrative and a character within it. In other words, he is fully implicated in the story on both sides of the curtain: he not only appears on stage himself, but also sits in the prompter's box, whispering their lines to each of the other characters. First by the Prefect, then by Dupin, events and conversations are recounted to the narrator, who then relays them to the reader, with the result that, as and while he speaks in his own voice, the narrator operates throughout as a kind of mobile framing device. And in turn the narrator's 'own' voice, so to speak, is itself implicitly surrounded by a silent, invisible, supplementary frame belonging to what, in an essay of 1964 whose significance for Derrida is hard to overestimate, Blanchot calls *la voix narrative*: i.e., the narrative, or, perhaps better, narrat*ing* voice (compare *AT*, 72; 153).[46]

In Blanchot (differently to what it usually means in narratology), the term refers not to the narrative voice as delegated to this or that character in the story (as in the case of 'The Purloined Letter', for instance), nor to the actual voice of an anonymous omniscient narrator (of the kind found, say, in *Bleak House* or *Middlemarch*), but to the prior possibility of a narrating voice, before that possibility comes to be identified with this or that specific narrator. And in so far as it raises the curtain upon the scene of narration, and sets the possibility of story-telling in motion, the narrating voice, in Blanchot's sense, is an indispensable precondition of any story, and always at a distance from the telling of the story, just as the frame around a picture is *both* a part *and* not a part of the picture it presents but also interrupts. 'The narrat*ing* voice', Blanchot explains, 'which is inside only to the extent that it is outside [i.e. exactly like a frame], at a distance without distance, cannot embody itself: whether it takes on the voice of a judiciously chosen character, or even (this voice that ruins all mediation) creates the hybrid function of mediator, it is always different from whoever or whatever utters it: it is the indifferent-difference that disrupts the personal voice. Let us (for amusement) call it spectral, ghostlike.'[47]

No narrative, then, is ever closed. Every narrator or narrative voice is always shadowed by a supplementary double. What this means, as 'La Folie du jour' shows, is that beginnings and endings of stories are never beginnings or endings in any rigorous sense, but simply provisional edges or borders which, rather than closing the text to the outside, do the very opposite. 'The Purloined Letter' is no stranger to this irremediable state of affairs, and it is not for nothing, Derrida suggests, that the tale therefore begins in Dupin's 'little back library, or book-closet', and concludes with a quotation from the eighteenth-century playwright Prosper-Jolyot de Crébillon. At both start and finish of the tale, the reader is dispatched on a journey through words and through texts which is in principle infinite, and from which he or she may never return, though the insistent reference to the number three in the address attributed to Dupin in the opening sentence (on the third floor at N° 33 rue Dunôt, which the reader might indeed know to be a fabrication) may be invitation enough for the reader to realise in passing that 'The Purloined Letter' was the third fictional outing of Poe's detective, whose powers of reasoning and imagination had already been smartly documented in two earlier texts by Poe, 'The Murders in the Rue Morgue', and 'The Mystery of Marie Roget', which were both worth a visit, and whose relevance to the present story was such that the outer contours of 'The Purloined Letter' were less certain than it might at first appear (*PC*, 512–13; 484–5).

If beginning and ending of 'The Purloined Letter' were not what they seemed, the same also applied to the two so-called triangular scenes on which Lacan based his interpretation. There, too, a spectral other stood silently ghosting or ghost-writing the text, splitting apart Lacan's repetitive Oedipal triangles, adding an always supplementary fourth wall, fourth side, or fourth dimension. Beyond the triangles imposed by Lacan what counted more, on Derrida's submission, were the doubles, and doubles of doubles populating Poe's story, from the 'twofold luxury of meditation and a meerschaum', with which the tale begins, to the double identity (both 'poet *and* mathematician', writes Poe) of Dupin's duplicitous double, D— , with whom it ends, and including all that occurs, at least twice over, between these two points (*PC*, 511–24; 483–96).[48]

It was here that Derrida once more encountered Freud, not so much the Freud who had inspired so much biographical psychoanalytic criticism (though, as Derrida pointed out, there were aspects of Poe's writing noticed by Bonaparte of which there was no mention in Lacan, including, notably, the involvement of the narrator (*PC*, 487–8; 459–60)), but the Freud of the later essay on 'The Uncanny' from 1919, devoted in part to the theme of the double in E. T. A. Hoffmann. In that paper what Freud had begun to address more explicitly was the strange, disquieting reversibility of the *heimlich*, i.e. familiar or homely, into the *unheimlich*, i.e. uncanny or eerie, of that which began inside (in the unconscious), but manifested itself outside (as hallucination), before crossing once again in the opposite direction. In the process, what became increasingly apparent for Freud was the porous nature of these boundaries. Needless to say, Freud's interest in the uncanny was significantly rekindled, as *Beyond the Pleasure Principle* suggests, by his growing awareness of the deathly, machine-like uncontrollability of repetition, and it is no exaggeration to say that here is where deconstruction, in a way, began – without ever beginning as such.[49]

For his part, Lacan was anything but unaware of Freud's inquiry into repetition and the compulsion to repeat. Oddly enough, however, there is no explicit mention of Freud's paper on 'The Uncanny' in the Seminar on 'The Purloined Letter', which, from the outset, is content to dismiss the products of the imagination, including such fantasies as that of the double, as mere 'shadows and reflections'.[50] Here, perhaps, lies the nub of the divergence between Lacan and Derrida in reading Freud and much else besides. Everything turns on two rather different accounts of chance and repetition. For Lacan, as his reading of 'The Purloined Letter' testifies, there was an order, a direction, a sense to repetition, which is why, whatever accidents befell the letter in the story, its final destination, for Lacan, could not *not* be what it was. Chance, in the end, and from the outset, had abolished itself, dialectically, and turned itself into ineluctable necessity. This was Lacan's famous conclusion. 'What is said or meant by the "purloined" letter, or indeed by any letter still "pending" ["*en souffrance*": this is a letter that, like a symptom, is suffering from not yet having been delivered]', he wrote, 'is that a letter always arrives at its destination.'[51]

Does it matter whether the necessary destination of the letter is determined prospectively or retrospectively? Slavoj Žižek, the Lacanian cultural critic, for one, seems to think so, claiming, he writes, that 'Lacan's exposition of the way a letter arrives at its destination *lays bare the very mechanism of teleological illusion.*' Citing the so-called 'limit case of a letter *without* addressee', i.e., that of 'a message in a bottle thrown into the sea from an island after shipwreck', Žižek goes on to argue that, for the Lacanian analyst, the 'true addressee is namely not the empirical other which may receive it or not, but the [Lacanian] big Other, the symbolic order itself, which receives it *the moment the letter is put into circulation*, i.e., the moment the sender "externalises" his message, delivers it to the Other, the moment the Other takes cognizance of the letter and thus disburdens the sender of responsibility for it.'[52] Žižek's objection is characteristically forthright. It serves in fact, however, only to support Derrida's case, for so long as the destination of the letter is construed as a place of truth (the 'true addressee', Žižek calls it), the circle of exchange as a closed circuit, and the identity of the addressee as an essential, non-empirical property of the letter, identified here as the Lacanian big Other, i.e., the place of language and sense itself, so it would seem to follow that the letter in Žižek's bottle cannot actually ever get sent at all, but has always already been received by its transcendent addressee, who, knowing what it says, cannot therefore in fact read it. In the end, then, for Žižek as for Lacan, chance is secret necessity, repetition unavoidable fate, and the signifier destiny.[53]

True enough, for Derrida too, chance was necessity: but in a radically different sense. From Derrida's perspective, Mallarmé's titular proposition that 'a throw of the dice will never abolish chance' remains irreducible. Chance, being irremediable, can never be overcome. So while for Lacan a letter always reaches its destination, for Derrida, by contrast, it is necessarily always possible for the letter *not* to reach that destination. Derrida went further. If any letter is to arrive at its destination, as sometimes though not always happens, it can only be, he reasoned, because it may always *not* arrive at that destination. It is '[n]ot that the letter never arrives at its destination', Derrida explains, 'but it is part of the structure of the letter that it is capable, always, of not arriving. And without that threat . . . , the circuit of the letter would not even have begun. But with that threat, it is always possible for it *not* to be completed' (*PC*, 472; 444; translation modified). Derrida goes on: 'a letter *does not always* arrive at its destination, and from the moment this possibility is part of its structure, it may be said that it never truly [*vraiment*: i.e. really, and in truth] reaches it, that when it does reach it, this possibility-of-it-not-reaching-its-destination exposes it to the constant worry of internal drift' (*PC*, 517; 489; translation modified). If a letter remains undelivered, still suffering in the mail, as Lacan puts it, then it may be that the letter knows it will never properly, wholly, truly arrive where it is meant to, even when, as sometimes happens, it does indeed arrive after all at the correct address.

Readers will remember that Derrida has recourse to much the same argument in considering Austinian performatives. The iterability governing the possible success of performatives, he suggested, was the same iterability as that which presided over their possible failure. Both outcomes belonged together, and one could only divorce the chance of the one from the prospect of the other by dogmatic fiat. The same, according to Derrida, applied to the postal system. The possibility a letter might go astray is an inevitable concomitant of any letter being delivered at the correct address, not simply because accidents always happen, as they do, but, more essentially, because no message can be addressed without risking being misaddressed, sorted without being missorted, or delivered without being misdelivered, and so on. Indeed, as in the case of the intimate postcard I mistakenly send to my mother, it may not even always be possible to say where the one ends and the other begins, and it may be perhaps that the card was also destined for my analyst, unless it was simply a fragment, since deleted, from my book on Derrida. The circuit of possibility, of reading and misreading, of direction and misdirection, by definition, cannot be closed. Any one address always already includes the possibility of all other addresses, including no address at all, and vice versa, and the message is therefore left to drift according to the hazardous logic of destinerrance: the necessary possibility that any message may go astray, i.e. that it will sometimes arrive as intended, but that, in so far as this outcome can never be guaranteed, it will never wholly or entirely arrive at that place, but will always be liable to be diverted, re-routed, or simply lost. Or perhaps fished out of Morecambe Bay to the relief and consternation of a shipwrecked psychoanalyst.

Any postcard, then, can always be read, deciphered, purloined, appropriated, even destroyed by someone for whom it was not originally intended, and each of these possibilities is inseparable from the structure of all postcards in general. If matters were otherwise, there would be no postcards. If I can write on this postcard which I am mailing from foreign parts my fervent desire for my significant other, then those words can be read not only by myself and my lover, but also by the postman or my neighbour; and if it were not possible in principle for the postman or my neighbour to read those private thoughts, and make of them what they will, then it would not be possible for my significant other, let alone myself, fondly to peruse them either. True, those works may perhaps be written in code, like the postcards cited by Derrida in the opening section of *The Post Card*, but this would not alter the essential structure of the exchange, merely make interpretation of the card more difficult. For what would be a code that had no cipher, since even a code known only to one person, in so far as it was a code, could in principle be reconstructed and made available to all? Remember Linear B. And whatever applies to postcards also holds for all other forms of communication in general, including letters, sealed and unsealed, faxes, emails, encrypted or not . . .

As soon as there was repetition, Derrida argued, authority was compromised, property or propriety impaired, and destination derailed. Whenever there was repetition, in other words, there was text, and whenever there was text, there was something more, something other, something perpetually divisible, like the frame, that exceeded the simple opposition of presence and absence associated by Lacan with the signifier and that signifier of the signifier, the phallus. And while the phallus in Lacan was always either present or absent, present while being absent, absent while being present, implying, among others, that the other sex was only ever construed as the negative reverse image of male sexuality, so in Derrida the movement of writing was such as to be always irreducible to any of the fixed positions implied by these binary alternatives. Lacanian theory, Derrida contended, was not just a logocentrism, privileging the spoken word over writing, but a phallogocentrism too, subordinating sexual desire and sexual differences to negativity: to absence, lack, castration. Dissemination, on the other hand, argued Derrida, was not bound by any such horizon. It was itself already the law: in its folly, its excess, its otherness. This was not to say dissemination turned aside from psychoanalysis, which already had it running through it. And in his own reading of Poe, far from dispensing with psychoanalysis, Derrida sought instead to enlist its radical power in order precisely *not* to position literature or desire as such, and place them under the jurisdiction of truth.

The exchange between Derrida and Lacan did not end here. Derrida, for his part, while continuing to pay tribute to the originality and importance of Lacan's return to Freud, was also careful to underscore the irreducible divergences between Lacanian theory and deconstruction (*R*, 57–88; 39–69). Lacan's reply was more circuitous. In May 1976, some months after the first publication of 'Le Facteur de la vérité' in the journal *Poétique*, in the course of a seminar series devoted in part to James Joyce and knot theory, in particular the theory of Borromean rings, Lacan made what some may take to be a final attempt to return Poe's perhaps wrongly delivered, still pending, suffering letter to its rightful owner, and observed as follows: 'Truth to tell', he said, 'the Borromean knot completely changes the meaning of writing. It gives writing an autonomy which is all the more remarkable because there is another kind of writing, resulting from what might be called a precipitation of the signifier. That is where Derrida laid the emphasis, but it is entirely clear that I showed him the way.'[54]

The remark explains, at least in part, Derrida's opening words at the 1990 Lacan conference mentioned earlier, where he began his closing contribution not by asking but exclaiming: 'What isn't Lacan supposed to have said! What won't he have said!' (*R*, 57; 39; translation modified).

## Yes yes

Few bodies of writing are as imposing or distinctive as the work and works of James Joyce, whom Derrida first read in the United States in the mid-1950s. The encounter was an important one. Derrida himself testified as much as early as 1962 in the course of a brief but much noticed digression in his *Introduction to Husserl's 'Origin of Geometry'* which gave Joyce the distinction of being the first literary author to be discussed by Derrida in print (*OG*, 104–5; 102–3). In the two decades that followed, Derrida made several further fleeting or oblique references to Joyce (*UG*, 29–34; *PSJ*, 150–2), including for instance the enigmatic footnote in *Dissemination* declaring 'the whole' of 'Plato's Pharmacy', 'as readers will not have been slow to notice'(!), to be 'merely a reading of [or *by*, says Derrida] *Finnegans Wake*' (*D*, 99; 88; translation modified), or, in more sustained yet still elliptical fashion, the various entries dealing with Joyce's legacy in *The Post Card* (*PC*, 154–5, 161, 255, 257–8; 141–2, 148, 238–5, 240–1).

In the France of the 1960s and 1970s Derrida was not alone in returning to Joyce, and his concern for the writer's work coincided with a widespread renewal of interest on the part of the literary avant-garde. But it was not until the early 1980s that Derrida took the opportunity to develop his reading more explicitly. This he did in two rather different presentations devoted in turn, in necessarily partial fashion, to *Finnegans Wake* and to *Ulysses*. The first paper, improvised on the basis of notes at a Joyce conference in Paris in 1982, and the more tentative of the two, was entitled 'Deux mots pour Joyce' ('Two Words for Joyce'), and was mainly concerned with the issue of (un)translatability in *Finnegans Wake* (*UG*, 15–53; *PSJ*, 145–59). Derrida's second piece, 'Ulysse gramophone' ('Ulysses Gramophone') (*UG*, 57–143; *A*, 256–309), was more ambitious, and written in response to an invitation by the James Joyce International Symposium to deliver the opening keynote address at their annual conference in Frankfurt in June 1984. It took as its topic the trace of 'yes' in *Ulysses*: not only the word itself, and the letters it contained, but, more fundamentally, the performative and more-than-performative structure it embodied.

In 1962, discussing the relationship between language, history, memory, and culture, Derrida had placed Husserl and Joyce at opposite ends of a spectrum. Whereas Husserl, in order to think the possibility of history, had put actual history into parentheses in order to drill down to the purity of univocal meaning, Derrida argued, so Joyce had set about rousing himself from the nightmare of history, in Stephen Dedalus's famous words from *Ulysses*, via the opposite route, that is, by dint of a massive, totalising accumulation of myth, knowledge, literature, and languages, as *Ulysses* and *Finnegans Wake*, each in their differing ways, bore witness. As Derrida put it in 1994, 'Joyce wanted to make history, the resuming and the totalisation of history, possible through the accumulation of metaphoricities, equivocalities, and tropes. Husserl, on the other hand, thought that historicity was made possible by the transparent univocity of language. There is no historicity without the transparency of the tradition, Husserl says, while Joyce says there is no historicity without this accumulation of equivocality in language' (*DN*, 26).

The Joyce that first emerged in Derrida's reading, which was to remain relatively unchanged even in the later texts, was that of an author, not unlike Hegel, having at his disposal here and now the total sum of existing historical and cultural knowledge, embodied in an infinite array of actual and virtual languages. As a consequence, the question that confronted all readers of Joyce, though Derrida does not quite formulate the argument in this way, was the exact same question of the frame at stake in his readings of Mallarmé, Blanchot, and Poe. For faced with the encyclopaedic inexhaustibility of *Ulysses* or *Finnegans Wake*, what position or place was it possible for a reader to adopt? Well might *Finnegans Wake* be famously addressed to 'that ideal reader suffering from an ideal insomnia',[55] this served merely to exacerbate the difficulty of knowing what it might mean properly to read Joyce's text.

Expressed in those terms, the dilemma was insurmountable. It nevertheless provided Derrida with a toehold. Having reminded himself and his listeners in 1982 that Joyce was a writer he had long been actively reading, Derrida interrupted himself to ask a simple but far-reaching question.

> I don't know whether one can actually say 'I read [or am reading] Joyce' as I just have. Of course, one can only ever read [or be reading] Joyce, whether one is aware of it or not. That's his force. But statements like 'I read Joyce', or 'go read Joyce', or 'have you read Joyce?' have always struck me as irresistibly comic. It was Joyce who wanted people to laugh, and laugh out loud when faced with sentences of this kind. What do you mean exactly by 'reading Joyce'? Who can boast of having 'read' Joyce?'
>
> (*UG*, 24; *PSJ*, 148; translation modified)

Such questions were not only a function of the intimidating power and comprehensiveness of the Joycean corpus. They also raised, in unusually acute fashion, the question of what it means to be a reader or critic of any literary text. The scale of Joyce's work is certainly monumental. Any reader, in order to get to grips with the text, is forced to bring to reading a significant amount of specialised cultural, literary, and linguistic knowledge. It is hard, if not impossible, in other words, to read Joyce naively and innocently. With Joyce, then, Derrida acknowledges, it is always already too late (*UG*, 15; *PSJ*, 145). But if reading Joyce is specialised business, as universities seem to acknowledge (and this is where what is true of Joyce may be thought to apply to all literary texts in general), what skill or training is required to become a competent Joycean? How far does such competence extend, and what are its limitations? And what is the source of its authority and power to decide, evaluate, and pass judgement? For 'Joyce' is not a stable object that may be delimited and positioned as such, but an unparalleled singularity, bearing a unique, irreplaceable signature – of which it is legitimate to ask whether it is at all susceptible to theorisation by any specialised agency or committee of experts. And in any case is it not arguable that the encyclopaedic inclusiveness of Joyce's own writing makes any reader's efforts redundant? What is there to add to *Ulysses* or *Finnegans Wake* that is not already announced, included, and exhausted within these texts?

These are crucial questions, having profound implications for the future not only of literary criticism, but also of those institutions, notably universities, to which literature's future is increasingly bound, but which can never lay exclusive claim to any text. All was a matter of framing for critic and writer alike. For if there was a question as to how any so-called competent reader might frame Joyce's writing, staying outside it, so to speak, so as not to fall inside it, the same no doubt also held for Joyce himself. If it was true that *Ulysses* and *Finnegans Wake* had succeeded in framing, in truly encyclopaedic fashion, the whole of Western culture and history, obliging any reader in turn to assimilate that knowledge in order to read, how was it possible for Joyce himself, having finished his circumnavigation of the known textual universe, to lay claim to the novels that were his and stamp his signature upon them, much as a painter might affirm a canvas to have been completed by his or her hand by inscribing within the frame or outside it, sometimes even in place of the frame itself, something that was recognisable as the artist's signature?

Not for nothing perhaps had Joyce already famously imagined the artist in *A Portrait of the Artist As A Young Man* as a detached signatory to the work, 'like the God of creation, remain[ing] within or behind or beyond or above his handiwork, invisible, refined out of existence, indifferent, paring his fingernails'.[56] But though an author might profit from this association with divinity, it made the issue of the writer's position more difficult still. The question remained, as Derrida had rightly surmised in 1962: how to sign off the entirety of past history and culture without being engulfed by it? How to end history's nightmare, in other words, without becoming one of its casualties? Here, the logic of the frame became more unforgiving than ever. For it was plainly impossible to do the one without doing the other. To be outside was already to be inside. But with what consequences for literature and for criticism?

The question of signatures had long been a centre of concern for Derrida. In 1971, in 'Signature Event Context', he made the point that for any signature to function as a form of authentification, it was necessary for it to be iterable, i.e., repeatable and recognisable as both same and other. But what this implied was the necessary possibility that the signature could be produced in the absence of the signatory or by mechanical means, and might therefore *not* be authentic after all. If the signature guaranteed identity, then, it did so only at the cost of making identity theft possible too, with the inevitable rider that all claims to identity, by definition, could therefore not *not* be haunted by the threat of forgery. No signature, then, was ever quite what it claimed, and there is little doubt that, as he developed this argument, never far from Derrida's thoughts, standing alongside the sometime postman Shaun, his brother, double, and rival, was the Joycean figure of Shem the Penman ('a sham and a low sham'), forger and false-letter-writer par excellence.[57]

For Derrida, increasingly throughout the 1970s the question of the signature became inseparable from that of writing in general and literary writing in particular. In *Glas*, for instance, and the essay *Signéponge* (*Signsponge*), written the following year, devoted to the French poet Francis Ponge, Derrida suggested that the treatment of the signature by a text might be one criterion for differentiating philosophical writing from its literary counterpart (though the layout of *Glas*, consisting of two parallel columns of text, the one reading Hegel and the other Genet, and constantly overlapping in the process, did much to unsettle the idea that literature and philosophy might be presented as two neatly contrasted opposites). The philosopher Hegel, reasoned Derrida, writing in the left-hand column, had done everything possible to efface any suspicion of contingency from his work, including all evidence of his autobiography, which might prove an obstacle to the presentation of universal conceptual knowledge. To sign, Derrida argued, was to take a risk. 'In order to sign', he explained in *Signéponge*, 'it is necessary to arrest [*arrêter*: stop or interrupt] one's text, and no philosopher will have signed his text, decidedly, and singularly, nor spoken in their own name, accepting all the risks that involves.' 'Every philosopher', he went on, 'refuses to acknowledge the idiomatic character [*l'idiome*, i.e. that which makes it specific rather than universal] of his or her name, language, or circumstances, and speaks in necessarily improper concepts and generalities' (*S*, 31–2; 32–3; translation modified).

Not so Francis Ponge, however, Derrida maintained, and not so Jean Genet, the subject of Derrida's right-hand column. Genet, born in 1910 of an unknown father, given up by his mother at an early age to become a ward of the French Republic, the author (among others) of *Journal du voleur* (1949) (*The Thief's Journal*), and an unrepentant homosexual and sometime convict, too, had attempted the exact opposite. 'Moving silently, laboriously, minutely, obsessionally, compulsively, passing like a thief in the night', wrote Derrida, Genet 'deposited, so to speak, his signature where all the stolen objects used to be. In the morning, expecting to recognise the things you know, you keep coming across his name everywhere, writ large, small, in full or in short, distorted or reinvented' (*Gl*, 50–1b; 41–2b; translation modified).

Genet in his writing, then, appropriated everything of which he spoke, stealing words from the upright, so-called law-abiding, heterosexual establishment and making them secretly his own. This was no metaphor. In his novels, plays, and autobiographical texts, knowingly or not, Genet had carefully retraced the complex associations of his given family name, bequeathed to him alongside little else by his mother, in which it was possible to detect the common nouns *genêt* (broom or gorse) or *genet* (a small horse of Arabic or Spanish descent), with the result that, in such texts as *Notre-Dame-des-Fleurs* (*Our Lady of the Flowers*) or *Miracle de la rose* (*Miracle of the Rose*), Genet's numerous references to flowers or blooms, especially yellow ones, or even simply to the colour yellow itself, not to mention, added Derrida, the 'little continuous spurts' of the rider on his mount described in the opening pages of *Notre-Dame-des-Fleurs* (*Gl*, 31b; 24b; translation slightly modified), all took on the status of coded, cryptic signatures, turning each of those texts, among others, into a series of monumental statements embodying, preserving, eulogising or lamenting the other, the mother, and the writer himself.

In *Ulysses*, in his own inimitable fashion, Joyce had done something similar. The twenty-four-hour time frame utilised in the novel, published in 1922 on the occasion of author's fortieth birthday, took the reader back to 'Bloomsday', 16 June 1904, the date of Joyce's first walking out with Nora Barnacle. This secret incorporation of Joyce's autobiography within the fictional text bearing his name was no mere external circumstance. For one thing, it resonated powerfully, too, with the famous scene in the novel where Leopold Bloom, having finished gazing longingly at Gerty MacDowell, looks to leave a further trace of his presence on the beach by writing in the sand, with the aid of a conveniently elongated stick, the key word: 'I', constituting a whole paragraph on its own, like a signature, followed soon after by the similarly detached inscription: 'AM. A.' At which point Bloom does indeed arrest his text, and, says Joyce, 'effaced the letters with his slow boot' and 'flung his wooden pen away'.[58]

'What's in a name?', Stephen Dedalus had asked some time earlier, in similar vein, while discussing names and ghosts in Shakespeare's *Hamlet*, only to answer his own question, observing tartly: 'That's what we ask ourselves in childhood when we write the name that we are told is ours.'[59] Was it entirely indifferent in this connection, one might ask, that Joyce's initials gave rise to a mischievously redoubled J, or that, while his forename evoked one of Jesus' brothers, his family name, said to derive from a Breton word meaning 'lord', also implied the joy of an imminent fall, that happy fault or *felix culpa* so prominent in *Finnegans Wake*? For readers of Joyce's novel, cryptic associations such as these are anything but unremarkable, and represent but a tiny drop in the 'hitherandthithering waters' of Joyce's text, which flows this way and that with a multitude of anagrams, pseudonyms, and homonyms, signing itself now one way, now another, and always adding numerous new proteiform extensions to Joyce's initial, cipher-like characters, HCE and ALP, and including everybody and everything in-between and more, from Howth Castle and Environs to Haroun Childeric Eggeberth to H. C. Earwicker to Here Comes Everybody, from Anna Livia Plurabelle to Alma Luvia, Pollabella, and so on, and so on, and so on.

There was however a snag, a felicitous-infelicitous irony. 'O fortunous casualitas!', *Finnegans Wake* called it.[60] Each signature deposited in a work, in whatever form, immediately fell subject to the law of iterability. It could not *not* be exposed to *destinerrance*: the necessary possibility that the signature continue to be readable by others, in my absence, without the guarantee of my presence, and beyond my control. Any attempt on my part to appropriate language for myself or for my artwork could only result in my own expropriation by that language. The desire properly to sign a text necessarily ends in failure. Failure here, however, is also back-handed proof of success. For if it were possible for anyone literally to make language their own, then neither the novels and plays of Genet, nor the fictions of Joyce, nor indeed any writing at all would be possible, for words would not allow it. No monument could therefore be erected, Derrida repeatedly quipped in *Glas*, once again deploying the argument of the girdle, without that tomb (or *tombe*, in French) immediately falling (*tomber*, to fall). A funeral, wrote *Finnegans Wake*, using a similar double-edged pun, was properly and improperly, by necessity and by chance, inevitably and fortunately: a 'funferal' (fun for all), a waking of the dead that was also an awakening of the dead.[61] Here, Bloom's gesture in effacing his own incomplete sentence from the sand was more affirmative and knowing than it might at first appear. Erasure was a necessary function of any trace. In a sense it had already happened: 'Some flatfoot tramp on it in the morning. Useless. Washed away.' But that effacement remained, like a textual trace, a vestige of what, like a token of the future, having never been properly present, might yet return, like the sea, not as itself but something other: 'Tide comes here a pool near her foot. Bend, see my face there, dark mirror, breathe on it, stirs. All these rocks with lines and scars and letters.'[62]

Joyce's writing, then, was marked by what Derrida called a strange kind of madness, 'that madness of writing by which whoever writes effaces himself [or herself: Derrida's French is gender-neutral] even as he [or she] leaves behind, in order to abandon it, the archive of their own effacement.' 'These last two words', Derrida explained, referring to the contradictory pairing of *own* and *effacement*, 'speak madness itself' (*UG*, 19; *PSJ*, 114; translation slightly modified). Any signature, writes Derrida, pressing the two meanings into a single twofold word, is a site of what he calls ex-appropriation. In Joyce, and in writing in general, there is a double status and double relation that makes each text, on the one hand, absolutely singular, attributable only to a uniquely given act of writing, but, on the other, necessarily subject to a law of impersonality, accessible as such to an infinite number of possible readings or interpretations.

In itself this argument is not necessarily new. Indeed, generations of literary critics have sought to resolve the enigmatic tension between the universality of appeal and the singularity of occasion that is the hallmark of any artwork by positing some force, often described as artistic genius, capable of reconciling the two. The puzzle however remains: what is it that makes Shakespeare Shakespeare? But if the question is unanswered, it is not because of the impenetrable nature of artistic genius, but the logic of ex-appropriation governing signatures. For this signature I claim to be mine, paradoxically enough, is mine only if it is *not* properly mine at all, only if I have relinquished control over it for others to inspect, read, or forge. Elsewhere, Derrida makes a similar point about cultural identity, which is what it is only in so far as it always differs from itself and is in fact not reducible to itself (*OH*, 30; 25–6; *DN*, 13). And the artwork too, rather than being the fully embodied self-expression of its signatory, is only ever what it is in so far as it is *not* what it is: improperly proper, properly improper. In order to explain what makes Shakespeare Shakespeare, then, it would be necessary to know who or what Shakespeare is, which is an impossible task, not least because what may properly be deemed to be Shakespeare's does not in fact belong to Shakespeare.

Derrida explores the paradox further by considering the related question of translatability. *Finnegans Wake* is a work that has often been portrayed, of course, for good reason, as a radically untranslatable, self-fulfilling, self-explicating, self-exhausting modernist work (which is not to say that attempts have not been made to translate it). As Derrida acknowledges, one of the immense challenges of the book is that Joyce's text is already composed in an incalculable number of actual or virtual languages, and that the movement of translation, having already started in the text, and showing no sign of ever coming to an end, has the potential to reduce the reader to little more than a passive spectator: overwhelmed, frustrated, even resentful. In so far as the novel came already equipped with its own reading, might it not then be argued that the book is unreadable? Or is there a point at which the totalising authority of Joyce's writing is interrupted, hesitates, and is forced to give way?

The issue is one that has particular pertinence for readers of Joyce. But this is not to say it does not have more general relevance for all acts of reading where, by definition, and before all else, the task of the reader is to subscribe to the terms of the text being read. But if so, how is interpretation possible? By way of response, Derrida points to the question of translatability. For if on the one hand everything in *Finnegans Wake* already enjoys its own multilingual translation, the same cannot be said for the movement of translation itself, as Derrida shows by citing the two unassuming words evoked in his 1982 title, 'he war', taken from the episode in *Finnegans Wake* recounting the erection and fall of the Tower of Babel.[63]

In that sentence, if it is a sentence, at least two languages battle for attention. 'He' belongs, it seems, to English, but 'war' to either English or German, making the boundary between the two a no-man's-land of contested territory. 'War' may refer to (English) hostilities; read alongside 'he', it may echo too with the phantom presence of words such as 'hear', 'ear', and so on, all of which reverberate powerfully, Derrida suggests, through the passage in which the phrase appears. But 'war' may also be (German) was, with overtones of 'wahr', true, which also retains some of the connotations of the verb 'bewahren', to keep or preserve, even as it may seem to want to swap its meaning with 'Ware', the word for merchandise, goods, or wares. There are other resonances too. For if interpretation is a battlefield, it is because language and languages are already at war with one another, and with themselves, so that as *Finnegans Wake* shows, time and again, each and every word is already itself and another, heavy with one meaning only in so far as it is pregnant with others.

Something however resists this perpetual movement of translation, while paradoxically also being what makes it possible in the first place: the war of language(s) itself. Any translation committed to rendering Joyce's multilingual phrase 'he war' into a single target language, which is the minimal condition any translation would need to fulfil if it is to be acceptable as a translation, can but fail in the face of Joyce's text. Not because Joyce's text may be thought to be richer in its original Babelian version, but because to ignore the multilingual virtuality of the phrase 'he war' by translating it into, say, French, German, Chinese, or even English, as one must, is not to translate it as a multilingual singularity. For the selfsame reason, then, *Finnegans Wake* is both infinitely translatable and absolutely untranslatable. It requires translation yet makes translation impossible; it demands to be translated yet refuses to be translated; the reader can but begin by attempting to translate Joyce's words, only then to be forced to give up in the face of their untranslatability. This is no isolated problem. As all readers of Joyce know, like readers of many other texts, ancient as well as modern, *Finnegans Wake* cries out to be interpreted, while obstinately doing everything in its power to defer, resist, and complicate interpretation. The predicament, though, Derrida argues, is not a function of the supposed modernism of *Finnegans Wake*. It is general and universal, and has to do with the fact that each and every text is singular: irreplaceable, untranslatable, iterable.

*Finnegans Wake* is unique, but does not stand alone. A similar effect of paradoxical untranslatability, achieved by a different route, may be found in a famous novel by Samuel Beckett, published in French in 1951 under the title *Malone meurt* and translated five years later by the author into his own Anglo-Irish as *Malone Dies*. In the novel, Beckett's narrator has occasion at one point to refer ironically to a famous Irish electoral slogan of the early 1930s which served at the time as an expression of opposition to the recently formed Irish Free State. The slogan was: 'Up the Republic!', and is cited as such, i.e. in English, in the original French text of Beckett's novel. In *Malone Dies*, however, the slogan is given, i.e. translated without being translated, as – 'Up the Republic!'[64]

From French text to English text, the words appear to be the same, and to that extent the words 'Up the Republic!' may be deemed to be an acceptable translation of the words 'Up the Republic!'. What Beckett omitted to translate, however, for the simple reason that it is impossible to do so, was the strangely foreign occurrence of the Anglo-Irish expression 'Up the Republic!', spoken no doubt in a cod French accent, in a French-language text. As Beckett's novel travelled from one language to another, the incongruity attaching to these perhaps incomprehensible Anglo-Irish words as they occur in a francophone context was erased. This was no isolated phenomenon. The same applied to the names used by Beckett in *Molloy*, *Malone Dies*, and *The Unnamable*, all originally written in French, but full of such foreign-yet-not-foreign names as Molloy, Moran, Malone, Mahood and the like, all of which figure in French as foreign bodies detached from that other, unavailable language of Anglo-Irish. As Beckett plainly realised, to have given the slogan in French translation in the original text of *Malone meurt*, or even, by way of compensation, to have given it in French in *Malone Dies*, as 'Vive La République!', say, would have been a total mistranslation, not only because of the different status of the Republic and Republican movement in France and Ireland, but also because of the precise historical connotations of the phrase 'Up the Republic!', not to mention the ghostly overtones of an untranslatable scatological pun. In sum, the English phrase 'Up the Republic!' appearing in an anglophone text cannot and does not translate what is said by the selfsame words 'Up the Republic!' appearing in a francophone text.

All Beckett could do is repeat the words, but in so doing, according to the logic of iterability, alter them, and repeat them as different from what they were. As in *Finnegans Wake*, then, the possibility of translation encounters a structural limit, which remains as a signature, i.e., a mark of language that is infinitely repeatable but entirely singular. True, it can always be divorced from its context, but it continues to carry with it the imprint of that context. No text, then, even when it is written in a single language, ever belongs wholly to that language, but always brings with it the possibility of every other language, past and future, as the story of Babel implies; and conversely each text, in so far as it is translatable at all, is also by that very token absolutely untranslatable.

Joyce and Beckett are limit cases. But what comes to be re-marked in their writing by the implicit or explicit pressure of another language or languages(s), Derrida argues, is necessarily already marked in all writing. The result is a double bind affecting not only translation but interpretation in general. For any conscientious reader has to confront two contrary requirements, both demanding to be fulfilled, and neither ready to yield to the other. On the one hand, says the text: 'Read, interpret, translate everything I say, using all available theories, protocols, or methods in so far as they can be applied with rigour and consistency.' 'Respect, however, my singularity', it says on the other, 'and know that I am irreducible, that my meagre words cannot be taken from me, even though I know them not to be mine.' 'Die Schrift ist unveränderlich', says the priest in Kafka's *Trial*, 'und die Meinungen sind oft nur ein Ausdruck der Verzweiflung darüber.' 'The text is immutable, and the opinions are often only an expression of despair over it.'[65] To read any text is to recognise there is always an unreadable, uninterpretable, untranslatable remainder, which is what makes reading at one and the same time possible and impossible. Without it, there would be nothing to read other than what has already been read, which is also to say that reading can only occur so long as there stands before it what it cannot assimilate or overcome: the unreadable.

The unreadable is nothing ethereal, transcendent, or theological. It is not beyond reading, but is what is inherent in all reading. Reading stands at a limit, and can only be grasped at that limit. The paradox is the same as with translation. For what is it that always remains to be translated, thereby supplying the proof of its non-present futurity, Derrida asks, if not that which it is impossible to translate? '[W]hat remains *untranslatable* [*intraduisible*: i.e. impossible to render in any other single language]', he explains, in a formulation that is itself at the limit of translatability, 'is at bottom the only thing there is to *translate*, the only thing *translatable* [*traductible*: i.e. which demands to be translated]. The to-be-translated [*l'à-traduire*] of that which is translatable [*du traductible*] can only be the untranslatable [*l'intraduisible*]' (*UG*, 59–60; *A*, 257–8; translation modified).

Derrida glosses this move further in a series of remarks on Walter Benjamin's famous essay 'The Task of the Translator' (*Psy*, 203–35; *DT*, 164–207). His purpose is to bind the translatability and interpretability of a text not to established past or current norms, but to the unpredictability of the future: a future which is 'à-venir', which cannot be dominated by any present, but is always forever still to come and endures as a demand never to be fulfilled. There is however nothing negative about the formulation, which is rather in the form of an affirmation that cannot be contained, restrained, or bounded within any horizon of power or possibility. This is why the future to come, Derrida insists, carefully distinguishing it from the future as a mode of deferred present, is literally im-possible, for it exceeds all my capability or capacity, on the basis of any programme of rules, regulations, or expectations, to subordinate, subjugate, or subjectify it.

The impossible in this sense is inseparable from everything that for Derrida raised an issue of responsibility. For to what do we owe responsibility more than anything else, he asks, if not to that for which we are in fact *not* responsible, and makes upon us an infinite demand? Is it not the case, too, he argues, pointing to the experience of post-apartheid South Africa, that the only thing worth pardoning is that which is in fact unpardonable? And in much the same way is not the only thing worth avowing that which is unavowable, the only thing worth remembering that which is already forgotten, and resists facile retrieval? For it was only at that fragile barely thinkable limit that it was possible beyond possibility to envisage the future at all, in its absolute otherness, as threat or as promise.

In Frankfurt in 1984 Derrida began by returning to the untranslatable fold implicit in all natural language(s). 'Oui, oui,' he told his audience, 'vous m'entendez bien, ce sont des mots français', a sentence that, rendered literally, may be translated: 'Yes, yes, you can hear me loud and clear, these are French words' (*UG*, 57; *A*, 256; translation modified). But the words in question having now become English ones, the absurdity of the sentence is immediately apparent. Other translations are possible, like the hybrid version preferred by Tina Kendall who writes: '*Oui, oui*, you are receiving me, these are French words' (*A*, 256). The awkwardness of the wording confirms Derrida's point, which was that because they were marked twice over, now used to mean something, now mentioned as part of a given language, without it being possible to divorce the one from the other, those words resisted proper translation. This was not to say that they were not repeatable or could not be quoted, on the contrary, as Derrida was at pains to demonstrate in the pages that followed. But their status was that of a signature: infinitely repeatable as always other than what it was, both demanding of translation yet absolutely untranslatable.

There followed a lengthy and often comic exploration, by turns witty and learned, of the uncanny capacity of Joyce's text to include within itself the whole of past history, as well as the reader's ability to reinterpret the words on the page in idiosyncratic manner. Joyce's signature, in other words, appeals to the reader's signature. To read a text, Derrida puts it, is to countersign it. The repeatability inhabiting both these signatures implies the intervention of chance: as both inescapable necessity and providential opportunity. At the heart of every text, something machine-like is at work, making it impossible to oppose organic wholeness to technological repetition. So it was, Derrida suggested, that much of this lecture on Joyce was dictated to him by the contingent circumstances of its writing. He began preparing the paper, he tells his listeners, while in Japan. This prompted him to start – since it is always necessary to start somewhere, in a place partly determined by chance – with a random reference in *Ulysses* to the 1904 battle of Tokyo.

Chance, while remaining incalculable, soon developed its own peculiar necessity, not unlike the Freudian unconscious, and Derrida's circumnavigation, miming that of Leopold Bloom, which itself was busily miming that of an ancient Greek traveller long ago, began to follow an unpredictable course, involving a visit to a hotel shop, a set of postcards, a garbled phone conversation, an inspirational accident, an unexpected encounter in the street, and much else besides. Calculation and incalculability are strange but inevitable bedfellows, and just as Joyce's writing was scrupulously planned yet ruled by chance, so Derrida's reading too fell subject to the irresistible machinations of *destinerrance*. There was, then, no alternative: if one was to read Joyce, even if one was to read at all, it is necessary to be responsive and responsible to this arrival of the unpredictable, uncontrollable other. No reading, even before it turns to assent or criticism, can begin other than by saying *yes* to the text.

This brought Derrida to his topic: yes. His interest in the word was in part a function of its eccentric yet fundamental grammatical status. Though it may be classed as an adverb and used sometimes as a noun, 'yes' is an unusual part of speech in so far as its meaning consists in affirming or reaffirming the act of speaking or writing as such from which it cannot be divorced. In so far as every act of speech implied an iterable signature, 'yes' was one of the marks of that signature. In this respect, 'yes' was not limited to the actual word 'yes', but implicit in all speaking and writing. Wherever speech or writing occurred, Derrida affirmed, the effect was always minimally and repeatedly to attest: yes, yes, I affirm, I agree, even to the point, Derrida went on, that saying 'yes' necessarily occurred before any ownership over 'yes' could be established. In other words, saying yes did not assume or accredit the prior existence of any subject or subjectivity. On the contrary, no such subject was even thinkable without the intervention of an always prior yes.

Though it differs from it in many ways, the *yes* in Derrida follows something of the same logic as the *il y a*, the *there is*, as found in the texts of Levinas or Blanchot (which already differs from one to the other). Like the *il y a*, yes does not appeal to any prior subjective or other ground. It is always already repeatable (yes, yes), as Derrida points out, always already the trace of a response to another (no-one says yes on their own, even if the person to whom one is replying is oneself). 'Before the *Ich* in the *Ich bin* either affirms or negates', says Derrida, referring to Joyce's inversion of Mephisto's famous line in Goethe's *Faust*: 'Ich bin der Geist, der stets verneint!' (i.e. I am the spirit that always negates or says no; Joyce described Molly Bloom as the spirit that always says yes), 'it poses or pre-poses itself: not as *ego*, the conscious or unconscious self, a masculine or feminine subject, spirit or flesh, but as a pre-performative force which in the form of the "I", for example, marks that "I" is addressing another, however indeterminate he or she may be: "Yes-I", or "Yes-I-say-to-the-other", even if *I* say *no* and even if *I* addresses without saying anything. The minimal primary *yes*, the "yes, hello" on the telephone, or the tapping on the prison wall, before meaning or signifying anything, marks: "I-here", listen, respond, there is a mark of some sort, there is something or someone else [*il y a de l'autre*: there is otherness]. Negativities may then follow, but even if they were to consume everything, the *yes* can no longer be erased' (*UG*, 126–7; *A*, 298; translation modified).

In so far as yes is always repeated, there are always two yeses. These however cannot always be told apart, and necessarily haunt or contaminate one another (*UG*, 108–9; *A*, 287). On the one hand, though it might never appear as such, yes marked the gift of language and languages, prior to the possibility of any economy of meaning, exchange, substitution, and return, inscribing itself as a singular, repeated signature, as rhythm, tone, music, laughter, and as a kind of supplementary quality attaching itself imponderably to every meaning: deferring, exceeding, displacing meaning(s) in general. The second yes was no less concerned with many of the same things, the crucial difference, however, was that repetition, in this context, was not a mark of dispersion or dissemination, but a sign of reappropriation, totalisation, mastery. Both yeses, Derrida suggested, traversed Joyce's text with exemplary power, constantly crossing or contaminating one another, with its laughter, for instance, operating now as a defiant gesture of textual omnipotence addressed to the reader, now as a sublime movement of overwhelming generosity, dispersing all positionality as such.

As a kind of double figurehead of these movements, both the totalisation of all meaning and the dissemination irreducible to it, Derrida elected the same tutelary spirit: Elijah. Elijah, first of all, was a name for the place, person, or voice in whom the memories, transformations, and textual transfers criss-crossing *Ulysses* all met. But Elijah was also a name for the unexpected visitor to whom a free slot had been allocated at this prestigious conference. Derrida's unspoken middle name, he reveals, was indeed Elijah, which confirmed him in his status as guest: not as Derrida but as someone always other than Derrida. For the name Elijah did not name any single individual, but announced the arrival of another, whose empty place was always set at table. This was Elijah: the always supernumerary participant and ghost of the future, without whom no reading could occur, and whose always imminent arrival, as promise or threat, with the one always implying the other, interrupted the stability of the present. Such too was the divided signature of Joyce's writing: turned towards the past and the future as a totalisation of all memory, but turned towards the future and the past as that which always held open the work for the arrival of the other. This accordingly was not Joyce's, but also Derrida's double conclusion:

The *yes* of memory, recapitulating mastery, and reactive repetition immediately doubles the fleet-footed dancing *yes* of affirmation, the open affirmation of the gift. Two responses or responsibilities, irreducible to one another, each relate the one to the other. Both sign, yet prevent the signature from being gathered up as one. They can only summon up another *yes*, another signature. Moreover, it is impossible to decide between two *yeses* that *must* resemble each other like twins, to the point of each being the copy of the other, the one as it were the gramophony of the other.     (*UG*, 141; *A*, 308; translation modified)

Derrida's paper was delivered to an audience of eminent Joyceans. Part of its purpose was to reflect on the viability of the institution of Joycean studies, which, in so far as it was founded less on unchallenged competence than on a shared commitment to Joyce's signature, was in the awkward position of not being able fully to constitute itself as itself without recourse to the intervention of another, a guest, so to speak, and presumed master theorist, who by coming from outside might recognise the institution and confer legitimacy on it. This, Derrida surmised, was the reason for his own invitation. He was only too aware, however, that, for general as well as particular reasons, he had no power to fulfil that role. The institution had no alternative but to confront its own precariousness: a precariousness that expressed itself in the unsatisfied need for external validation *and* the realisation no knowledge existed capable of matching the untranslatable, empty secrecy of Joyce's signature.

In this respect, the James Joyce Symposium, imposing institution that it is, was in no different a position to the massed ranks of commentators, critics, and students in general. They too could not *not* respond to the double bind inscribed in Joyce's work: the requirement that they countersign Joyce's text, in the knowledge, however, that each countersignature was only ever one in a lengthy chain of such responses extending into the future, of which all that might be said was that it was without end. The predicament is of course not peculiar to Joyce studies. It applies to the institution of literary criticism in general. For in so far as literature is itself an institution, and gives rise to the institution of literary criticism, so both institutions are fated to remain essentially illegitimate. Paradoxically, however, the illegitimacy of both literature and criticism is what gives both institutions not only the possibility but, more fundamentally, the obligation and the desire constantly to reinvent themselves in an ongoing movement bound, happily, to fail. Felix culpa! For it is the inability of literature and criticism to fulfil the goals they set themselves, that of exhausting whatever it is they are called upon to perform, which paradoxically ensures the future survival of both.

## Literature's secret

Common to all Derrida's writing on literary texts there is what the writer sometimes called his passion for literature. Although Derrida was pre-eminent among modern thinkers in taking the possibility of literature to be worthy of sustained philosophical attention, his purpose was never to produce a general theory of literature as such. Even when Derrida worked on a given authorial corpus, the object of scrutiny was never the totality of an author's work, but rather the inescapable and symptomatic stresses occurring at strategic points in that work. The point was not to subordinate specific texts to theory; it was more a matter of studying the limits of theorisation, what Derrida's friend, Paul de Man, a very different writer on literary questions, called the 'resistance to theory'.[66]

Derrida's passion for literature was less a fondness for playful aesthetic effects than an intense desire for an event of writing that might culminate in an affirmative critical encounter. Writing on Joyce, Celan, or Blanchot, Derrida did not claim to 'have "read" or proposed a general reading of those works'. What he did, he told Derek Attridge, was to write a text 'which in the face of the event of another's text, as it comes to me at a particular, quite singular moment, tries to "respond" or to "countersign", in an idiom which turns out to be mine' (*A*, 62). 'Almost never', he emphasised elsewhere, 'have I written about this or that author *in general* nor dealt with *the totality* of a corpus as though it were homogeneous. What for me is paramount is the distribution of forces and motifs in a given work, recognising what is hegemonic within it, or finds itself relegated to the margins, or is even denied. Here too I would always endeavour (as I strive to do on every occasion) to respect the idiom or the singularity of a signature' (*WT*, 20; 7; translation modified).

But no reading, any more than any signature, was ever purely private. In so far as both were bound by the logic of iterability, so Derrida's response to the texts he read raised wider philosophical, politico-ethical questions. There was no contradiction, as far as Derrida was concerned, between the singularity of the reading encounter and the universality of its implications. To read Mallarmé, Blanchot, Poe, or Joyce was not, for Derrida, to treat their writings as privileged models illustrating some general rule; it was rather to cite them as examples or counter-examples whose testimony served not to exhibit the law but to expose it, that is, show what it was while also exceeding it, revealing the counter-law of contamination and impurity inseparable from the law's very authority.

There was another reason for Derrida's preference for the marginal or borderline text. As far as literature was concerned, there was no absolutely self-identical object to be addressed by that name. But if there was no essence of literature, this did not mean there was not an institution called literature, whose conditions of possibility and evolving history needed investigation. On the contrary, it was precisely because literature had no autonomy or identity that it was possible for it to exist in and through history in a series of ever changing forms and contexts. As Derrida points out to Derek Attridge, 'if a phenomenon called "literature" appeared historically in Europe, at such and such a date, this does not mean that one can identify the literary object in a rigorous way. It doesn't mean there is an essence of literature. It even means the opposite' (A, 41).

If literature was an institution, Derrida suggested, it was an institution of a strange kind, without proper purpose or goal, and marked as a result by its enduring fragility and constant reinvention. It was an institution always on the brink of dissolution, Derrida observed in the same interview, 'a place at once institutional and wild, an institutional place in which it is in principle permissible to put into question, at any rate to suspend, the whole institution' (A, 58). As such, it corresponded to a set of structural possibilities and a series of changing historical circumstances. Between the two the relationship was dissymmetrical, which explains the remarkable persistence and yet strict unanswerability of the question: what is literature? 'The events known *by the name of literature* can be delimited', Derrida wrote in 1984. 'There is in principle', he argued, 'a possible history of that name and the conventions attached to its use. The same is not however the case for the structural possibilities of what has been given that name and is not limited to the events already known by that name' (Psy, 377; author's emphasis). On the one hand, then, in so far as it was writing, literature was governed by the conditions of possibility of all writing: *différance*, iterability, and what, in *Of Grammatology*, Derrida called the instituted trace ('Even before being bound to incision, to engraving, to drawing or to letters, and to a signifier referring in general to a signifier signified by it', he argued, 'the concept of graphy [*graphie*] implies, as the possibility common to all systems of signification, the instance of the *instituted trace*' (G, 68; 46)). But though *différance*, iterability, the instituted trace were indispensable for literature to occur, they were not in any sense specific to it, which was why the quest for literature's essential autonomy was bound to prove fruitless.

More specific to literature as such, on the other hand, Derrida argued, in so far as the word named a particular, albeit relatively recent historical phenomenon, were various legal principles and socio-political assumptions bound up with the history of the European legal system from the seventeenth or eighteenth century to the present. Without these, Derrida pointed out, literature in the modern sense was hard to imagine at all. Rather than the nature of poetic language, then, it was the law that was primarily responsible for determining what was right and proper to recognise as literature. In the essay 'Before the Law', dealing with Kafka's story of the same name, Derrida details the axioms, legal in origin, without which the institution of literature in the modern sense would be unsustainable. These were three in number. First, the law demanded of any would-be literary text that it be properly identifiable, whole in itself, distinct from all others, with a beginning and an ending, and belonging to a given, recognisable language: in a word, possessing and possessed of an authoritative and authorised title. Second, the law insisted that the text be attributable to a named, real-life author, whose intellectual property it was, and who was therefore legally responsible for it. And third, it was necessary, according to the law, that the text be classifiable by genre, so that it might be correctly located in the library. The presumption a text was part of literature, Derrida maintained, was on these conditions. This is not to say decisions were always unproblematic. For at every step there was room for undecidability (*Pr*, 101–4; *A*, 184–7).

The intervention of the law was not necessarily repressive. Fashioned in this way, literature no doubt benefited from these provisions. At any event, even today, it showed that literature was inseparable from a certain rule-governed socio-political environment, in which, for instance, intellectual property rights were more or less recognised, freedom of expression more or less protected, and the right to artistic licence more or less respected, which was also to say that literature, this precarious institution, was nothing neutral, but political through and through. For just like literature itself, the rights on which it depended were subject to controversy and contestation; and it was not by chance, following Blanchot, that Derrida should adopt as literature's emblem the famously embattled words of the Marquis de Sade's heroine Juliette, according to whom 'philosophy should say all [*doit tout dire*]'.[67] 'Literature', Derrida explained, 'is a modern invention, and is part of a series of conventions and institutions which, importantly, guarantee it in principle the *right to say all* [*le droit de tout dire*; author's emphasis]. In this way, literature binds its destiny to a certain kind of non-censorship, to the space of democratic freedoms (freedom of the press, freedom of speech, etc.).' 'No democracy without literature', Derrida concluded, 'no literature without democracy' (*Pa*, 64–5; 28; translation modified).

There was, however, a complication. Literature was inseparable from the right to say all, but the principle was at one and the same time a token both of literature's power and of its impotence. In any literary text what is said is always suspended. 'There is no literature', Derrida put it, 'without a *suspended* relation to meaning and reference' (*A*, 48). Again, this is not a property specific to literature, but the extension or generalisation of a trait of language apparent whenever words are scrutinised, commented upon, cited, or otherwise re-marked. Moreover, it was essential *not* to conclude, as Roland Barthes and other structuralist theorists were tempted to do, that literary language as such no longer referred to anything outside the artwork, or at best referred only to itself. This made no sense at all for Derrida, who had argued to very different effect in 'The Double Session' that reference or referral was in fact infinite, i.e., while it did not encounter a final referent, in whose embrace it might fall silent, nevertheless, and for that reason, it continued far beyond the uncertain confines of the work, far beyond its always provisional context, far beyond the whole of literature, past as well as future, restlessly scouring and exceeding the worldly horizon itself, and reaching, yet without ever ceasing, to the furthest limit of what it was possible or impossible to think. *Différance*, Derrida maintained, was anything but a theory of textual autonomy or reflexivity.

Rather than with any self-referential aestheticism the suspense or suspension evoked by Derrida had more to do with what, from 'The Double Session' onwards, he had advanced under the rubric of the undecidable or undecidability, which brought together at least four distinct motifs. The first was the irreducibility of any text to a given theme or set of themes, to any stable thesis, position, or positing. It was not that texts did not convey thematic meanings; rather that every text, in so far as it was a text, was always more or less than those meanings. There was, in other words, always a remainder. No text could be construed as fully present to itself, and was never wholly what it was without departing from itself. As Derrida suggests in *Glas*, both in particular and in general, apropos of Genet's novel *Pompes funèbres* (*Funeral Rites*):

> The rare force of the text is that you cannot catch it saying (and therefore limit it to saying): *this is that*, or, what amounts to the same thing, this is in a relationship of apophatic [*apophantique*: relating to knowledge achieved through negation] or apocalyptic [*apocalyptique*: revealed prophetically] unveiling, or has a determinable semiotic or rhetorical relationship with that, this is the subject, or is not the subject, this is the same, this is the other, that this is this text, and not that one, this corpus rather than that. There is still something else, something still other, always at issue. A rare force. At the limit, equal to zero. What might be called the potency of the text [*puissance du texte*: later Derrida will exploit the strange double meaning of the word *potence* that, both in English and French, implies both sexual power and the gallows, i.e. erection and castration alike].
>
> (*Gl*, 222–3b; 198–9b; translation modified)

This essential irreducibility of text to theme had a corollary: the irreducibility of any text to pre-emptive truth. This was the second main aspect of the undecidable. But it did not mean truth was somehow of negligible importance for Derrida. Nor was it to claim that all texts were by definition false, which was simply to reverse the question of truth without displacing or transforming it. It was to argue that truth, understood either as adequation between discourse and object, or as the self-presentation of the text, could not and did not command writing, control it in advance, and reduce all writing to a confirmation of what was thought to be the case or produced itself as truth. If writing was possible at all, Derrida argued, it meant that the value of what was true was not only infinitely complex, multiple, and shifting, but also was never given dogmatically in advance. The undecidable was not a concession to ubiquitous fictionality or to ideological relativism, but rigorous testimony to the necessary, but always provisional status of the limits, distinctions, and oppositions that are essential for thinking. It did not reflect a desire to annul or abolish differences, but was a response to the requirement that all conceptual and other distinctions be re-examined and reassessed critically if they were to be affirmed. It was Derrida's conviction that the limit passed everywhere, and that to insist on the undecidable character of the limit was anything but complacency; it was more like a call to think, and to always think further than the status quo allowed.

Here was the third important aspect of the undecidable, which Derrida was to underline increasingly in his later texts. Indecision, he insisted, was not bland indeterminacy, and did not, in any sense, correspond to a relativistic, liberally minded reluctance to take decisions (*L*, 273–5; 148–9). More radically, it was a necessary condition for all decision-making. There is nothing abstruse about this. Many of us, in everyday life, confront difficult moments of decision. Should I take this job? Should I sleep with this attractive stranger? Should I remain silent or tell the truth? If these dilemmas could be resolved, argues Derrida, by simple recourse to external authority, there would be no decision, merely the mechanical application of a belief system, moral code, or doctrine. For a decision to be both possible and necessary, there must be the undecidable, the hesitation between determined choices without which there would be nothing to decide. And even when there is a decision, the undecidable, as countless sleepless nights bear witness, never entirely disappears. Like the possibility things may always be otherwise, the undecidable continues to haunt each and every decision, which is thus never entirely final, and which, even though it may belong to the past, lingers on, as though it were still in the future, was never properly taken in the present, and has forever to be confronted, affirmed, underwritten, time and again.

This last point has often been misunderstood or sometimes wilfully misrep-resented by critics of Derrida, to the point of prompting him in some of his later work to consider abandoning the word *undecidable* itself, albeit not the crucial and enduring issues it served to identify. As he told an interviewer on French Radio in December 1998,

> I hesitate to use the word *undecidable* now because it has too often been interpreted, in ridiculous fashion, as paralysis, hesitation, or neutralisation, in the negative sense. For me, the undecidable is the very condition of any decision, of any event, and since you're referring to pleasure and desire, it is obvious that if I knew and could decide in advance that the other is indeed the identifiable other who is accessible to the movement of my desire, if there weren't always the risk that the other might be somewhere else, that I might have made a mistake, that my desire might not reach its destination, that the movement of love that I intend for the other might get lost en route or meet with no response, if there weren't this risk, marked with undecidability, then, there would be no desire. Desire is kindled on the basis of that indeterminacy which may be called the undecidable. So I think that, just like death, undecidability, or what I also call 'destinerrance', i.e., the possibility for an action not to reach its destination, is the condition of the movement of desire, which otherwise would expire before it happened. I conclude from this that the undecidable, and all the other values that may be associated with it, are anything but negative, paralysing or immobilising. For me it is exactly the reverse.    (*SP*, 52–3)

The undecidable, then, is inseparable from risk, and from the threat or promise of the future. It was thus closely related to questions of responsibility, not only with regard to the past or to the present, but also, even more acutely, with regard to the future. How to respond to the future, how to be responsible in the face of that which is necessarily unforeseen, unpredictable, uncontrol-lable, and unmasterable, and thus irreducible to established knowledge, moral doctrine, belief? These were questions that Derrida raised in relation to phi-losophy, politics, ethics, and much else beside. They had, however, particular pertinence in respect of whatever went by the name of literature. For if it was true, as Derrida argued, that literature had received as its birthright the pos-sibility of saying all, then the question that posed itself, for writer, reader, and critic alike, was the issue of responsibility. Was it legitimate, for instance, for a novelist to depict violence, rape, murder? To whom or to what was a writer responsible? And where did responsibility begin or end?

Derrida's response, rather than answering in any absolute manner, was to displace the terms of the argument. Censorship, he agreed, was not an answer;

but it was also imperative to examine each context in detail, carefully scrutinise its heterogeneity, and weigh up the always complex balance of opposing forces. In particular, any coherent analysis would need to recognise the undecidability implicit in all textuality and take account of the specific relationship between literature and responsibility. For if literature was inseparable from the possibility of saying all, then, as the history of literary censorship shows, this could not *not* bring literature into conflict with this or that body of authority, whether church, party, state, or dominant opinion, whose reaction would usually be to declare a given literary text to be irresponsible, guilty, or objectionable. But this did not mean that from this point on literature might be deemed responsible only to itself and to the aesthetic value of what it had to say, as writers in the late nineteenth or twentieth centuries had contended, if only to defend their own independence and freedom of speech.

Instead, argued Derrida, it was necessary to go beyond the sterile opposition between a responsibility to social norms, on the one hand, and aesthetic irresponsibility, on the other. First of all, if it was to remain true to the possibility of saying all, it was plain that literature had a responsibility *not* to obey established moral, religious, political, or other authorities. Admittedly, as far as dominant opinion was concerned, literature was always liable to appear irresponsible, if only as a direct consequence of the freedom it was intent on exercising. This did not mean that literature in itself, if it existed as such, was irresponsible, rather that it was the site of an exacerbated hyper-responsibility (*SP*, 24), which meant that issues of responsibility could neither be eluded nor resolved, and that, instead of being referred for final adjudication to this or that authority or body of opinion, they were best addressed instead to the more exacting tribunal of the future: the future of both reading and writing.

It followed from Derrida's remarks that the task facing any reader or critic was not to impose any moral, or ethical, or political, or other values on the text. This was not to ignore that there was a complex, oblique, tortuous, and sometimes tortured, physical relationship between writing and the ethical, and that, as Derrida puts it apropos of the poems of Francis Ponge, 'the instance of ethics [*l'instance éthique*: not ethics as established doctrine, but ethics in so far as it is a demand made upon me by an other or the other] is implicated bodily in literature [*travaille la littérature au corps*].' And this was why, Derrida went on, 'rather than *listening* to the lesson [Ponge] delivers', he said, 'I prefer to *read him*, that is, in so far as he delivers a lesson *about* morality, and not a moral lesson, *about* his genealogy of morals drawn [. . .] from a morals of genealogy' (*S*, 46; 52–3; translation modified). To read, in the text, was not to encounter familiarity, but strangeness, not conformist ideology, but the surprise of that which is unexpected and not bounded or framed by mere possibility, and which comes: from the future. 'Diversification', Derrida told an interviewer, 'is essential to deconstruction, which is neither a philosophy, nor a science, nor a method, nor a doctrine, but, as I have often said, *the impossible* and the impossible as *that which happens* [*ce qui arrive*: what comes or occurs, outside my control]' (*AA*, 20).

If literature was a passion for Derrida, then, it was not simply because it inspired or enthused him. It was rather that what was exposed in literature was the question of the future, a future irreducible to expectation or calculation and beyond the grasp of moral, political, ideological, or other norms. The object of Derrida's passion in this sense was not literature itself, assuming such a thing exists, and the charms and attraction of which it is capable, but something else buried within literature, always other than literature, which Derrida increasingly called: secrecy or the secret. As he explained in an oblique offering he was invited to write by David Wood:

> Perhaps I only wanted to impart secretly or confirm my (probably unconditional) liking for literature, more precisely for literary writing. Not that I love literature in general, and not that I prefer it to anything else, to philosophy, for instance, as is often thought by people who in the end cannot tell the difference between either. And not that I want to reduce everything to it, especially not philosophy. Literature, basically, is something I can do without, and without much difficulty, in fact. If I were to go live on a desert island, what I would most likely take with me would be history books or memoirs, which I read in my own way, even perhaps in order to turn them into literature, or the other way round, and this would be true for the other books too (art, philosophy, religion, humanities, natural sciences, law, etc.). But if, without loving literature in general and for itself, I do love something *in it* which is certainly not reducible to any aesthetic quality or any source of formal enjoyment, it may be said to be *in the place of secrecy* [*au lieu du secret*: *secret*, in French, is both a secret *and* secrecy]. In the place of an absolute secret. That is where the passion may be said to be. There is no passion without secrecy, this secrecy, and no secrecy without that passion. *In the place of secrecy*, where everything is nonetheless said and where the rest is nothing – other than the rest, and not even literature [Derrida is silently quoting the poet Paul Verlaine's proverbial line: 'and all the rest is literature']. (*Pa*, 63–4; 27–8; translation modified)

Why secrecy and the secret? Elsewhere, Derrida differentiates between two kinds of secret: the one, which already has an answer, which is therefore always on the point of being divulged, and is in that sense barely a secret at all; and the other, to which no answer can be given and which therefore cannot be revealed, which is therefore the only proper secret, albeit one that, resisting all discovery, is not properly a secret either, but nevertheless resists and remains as that which has never been present, cannot be made present, and remains perpetually separated from words as an always future possibility. The secret, then, is what is irreducibly singular, irreducibly other.

'Literature', Derrida told another interviewer, 'keeps a secret that does not exist, so to speak. Behind a novel or a poem, behind the riches of a meaning to be interpreted, there is no secret meaning to be sought. The secret of a character, for instance, does not exist, it has no depth outside of the phenomenon of literature. Eveything is secret in literature and there is no secret hidden *behind* it' (*AA*, 65). The word *secret* means: that which is separated, at a distance, inaccessible, and divided, other than what it may be. Its emblem, writes Derrida, was the word *perhaps*: intractable, indecipherable, futural.

What literature, deconstruction, for Derrida, have in common, then, is perhaps their joint commitment to what, reading Joyce, Derrida called the originary, redoubled yes. What both repeat, again and again, is a gesture of affirmation, turned not to the past, but to its future: to those countless, rigorous, inventive readings and writings of so-called literary and other texts that, happily, hopefully, haphazardly, are still to come.

# Chapter 4

# Reception and further reading

## Reception

In the course of an intellectual career lasting some fifty years and displaying throughout a quite remarkable persistence and inventiveness, Derrida radically transformed the contemporary philosophical, theoretical, and literary landscape as few others were able. For essential reasons, however, that were part of the purpose and manner of his writing, Derrida founded no school of thought, authored no official body of doctrine, fathered no philosophical institution that bore his name.

True enough, Derrida's signature was nothing if not singular, but no less than in the case of Joyce it could not, in so far as it was a signature, become a source of dogmatic authority, and at no stage was it ever presented by Derrida as such. Whatever Derrida sought to expound in his own name was by that very gesture exposed to the scrutiny of others. In this sense, Derrida's signature had more the structure of a gift, offered to readers, present and future alike, over which Derrida himself neither claimed nor sought to exert control. Moreover, like any signature, it was never wholly self-identical, but subject to constant variation, alteration, and transformation. This explained, among others, Derrida's often voiced desire, which was also a promise he endeavoured repeatedly to fulfil, to exploit and explore, at different moments in his writing, the widest possible range of discursive strategies, genres, tones of voice, and rhetorical or other forms.

But as in the case of all gifts and signatures, there was on Derrida's part a responsiveness and a responsibility to the other, both audience and text, which means his writing also places obligations on its readers, obligations that, on both sides, are inseparable from a shared fidelity to truth and a joint commitment to the affirmative gesture that was writing itself. The possibility (whether threat or promise) of misreading cannot of course be eliminated, and the dividing line between strong, innovative interpretation and misinterpretation is not necessarily one that is easy, or even desirable to enforce. What follows from this is not that readers are given licence to say anything whatever about a text (which, as any student knows, is always possible!), but almost exactly the reverse: it is to emphasise once again that reading is an infinite task, and that it is necessary to be ever more vigilant in interpreting a text, and that any reading owes it to itself to proceed by way of decisive, reasoned argument, even if the point to be made hinges on the undecidability in a text. All texts, then, require the most rigorous and most carefully sustained scrutiny that it is possible to bring to bear. As readers can verify for themselves, this is the key imperative that informs Derrida's own readings of canonic or non-canonic, philosophical or literary texts. What this confirms, and importantly so, is that, despite his reputation in the eyes of some, Derrida was no iconoclast seeking to discredit the legacy of Western philosophy, but a thinker who sought to remain faithful in his own way, beyond the temptation or expectation of blind faith, to that philosophical tradition.

When it comes to reading Derrida's own texts, the same principles demand to be applied. In paying relatively close, but always insufficient attention to a relatively small number of essays and articles by Derrida, this is what this book has sought to suggest: that, rather than appealing to certain ready-made or apparently self-evident concepts, it is necessary to begin by reading Derrida, reading his texts, patiently, at some length, in detail, and with as much attention as possible to their complex contextual history, in the secure knowledge that this contextual frame is happily multiple, cannot be exhausted, and is always susceptible to repetition and alteration. Admittedly, as Derrida acknowledges, his writing is not always easy to read, even less straightforward to translate, and seeks on purpose at times to challenge the competence of the audience. But this is not out of perverse disregard for the norms of academic discourse, which are in any case different in the francophone context to what is often standard in the Anglo-American academy, but because Derrida's writing, particularly in later texts, is minded to displace those conventions, and because the arguments he presents in his essays, articles, and seminar or conference presentations also demand that they be enacted in the very words used to explicate them. The difficulty of Derrida's writing, then, if it exists, is a measure not of his wilful obscurity, but unyielding rigour as a thinker. For that reason, it should perhaps best be seen as an effective stimulus to readers, who are enjoined to take the task of reading seriously.

From the outset, Derrida's thinking was the enemy of intellectual complacency, conformism, and blinkered submission to authority. In this regard, it is worth remembering that his work as a whole had little, if anything, to do with that largely non-existent theoretical movement sometimes given the meaningless, if not entirely vacuous name of 'French post-structuralism', a term never used by Derrida, or by any of his French contemporaries, which at its most basic corresponds to a rather dubious desire to gather up under one simplistic and erroneous label a wide range of divergent, and sometimes entirely incompatible bodies of work, by such thinkers as Foucault, Deleuze, Barthes, Derrida, Lyotard, Kristeva, and others. To assimilate Derrida (or indeed any of the other figures mentioned) to such a body of theory, generally identified as a bizarre concoction of historical and ethical relativism, obscurantism, and anti-rationalism, does little service to the cause of universal truth, in whose name this partial and partisan, and thoroughly erroneous description is often put forward. And the same goes for the similarly inaccurate description of Derrida as a postmodernist which prompted the following response by Derrida himself to a group of established Anglo-American Marxist critics in 1993:

> I am shocked by a certain haste with which *Specters of Marx* or my work in general is described as a simple sub-set, case, or instance of the 'genre' of *postmodernism* or *poststructuralism*. These are ragbag notions into which public opinion of the least well informed variety (and more often than not the mass-circulation press) sweeps more or less everything it does not like or understand, starting with 'deconstruction'. I do not consider myself to be either a poststructuralist or a postmodernist. I have often explained why I almost never use these words, except to say that they are inadequate to what I am attempting to do.
>
> (MS, 36; 228–9; translation modified)

The only purpose served by these common but misleading labels is distortion and obfuscation. Even the term 'deconstruction', which Derrida did accept as a provisional or partial description of his own work (and that of various others), named no single static or unified entity. It was essentially, and necessarily, diverse. If it could be characterised or defined at all, he insisted, it was not as a single, repeatable, applicable method or methodology, some programmatic strategy dominated by a final goal already visible on the horizon. Deconstruction more closely resembled a style, a way of reading and writing texts, addressing them with finesse, nuance, and all available sophistication, and with a different pen held, so to speak, in either hand. For what deconstruction demanded was an always double standpoint: on the one hand a rigorous, demanding, critical, but affirmative commitment to the legacy of the past, and on the other an equally exacting commitment to what the legacy of the past suppressed, remained unassimilated by it, and belonged perpetually to the future. '"To deconstruct" philosophy', he put it in 1967, 'is in this sense to think the structured genealogy of its concepts in the most faithful, internal manner, but at the same time, on the basis of a certain outside that cannot be qualified or named by philosophy, to determine what may have been concealed or excluded by that history, which became history by way of that repression, which, somewhere, was always a self-interested one' (*Po*, 15; 6; translation modified).

This was of course to place significant demands not only on Derrida's own thinking and writing, but also that of his readers, and it was probably inevitable therefore that, from quite an early stage, Derrida should find his work the object of controversy, inadvertent misunderstanding, or purposeful misrepresentation. In the superheated atmosphere of the Paris of the late 1960s and early 1970s, there was still broad consensus, at least within a certain philosophical establishment, in a phrase often attributed to Sartre, that Marxism remained 'the unsurpassable horizon of our time' (not that there was necessarily any agreement as to the consequences of the diagnosis), so it was not surprising that the first questions to Derrida were directed at him from that quarter. What was to be made, too, it was asked, of Derrida's declared interest in the thought of Heidegger, under suspicion then, as he was once more in the late 1980s, for his notorious involvement with Nazism during the 1930s? What was the relationship between deconstruction and history? Was the concept of writing compatible with dialectical materialism? What was the status of *différance* with regard to a Marxist – and, in the early 1970s, more specifically Maoist – dialectic of contradiction? These were the questions, among others, launched at Derrida in a long interview published in the avant-garde journal *Promesse* in 1971 (*Po*, 53–133; 37–96). And since this was the early 1970s, when hopes of reconciling Marx with Freud were on everyone's lips, there was another question, too: what was the position of deconstruction with regard to the psychoanalytic theory of the subject?

Patiently, as he did time and again later, Derrida unpacked his answers. The reading of Heidegger for which he was reproached was nuanced but unambiguous. On the one hand, deconstruction, he maintained, would not have been possible without a reading of Heidegger, and he acknowledged as much in 1967 (*Po*, 18; 9). On the other hand, this did *not* mean (and Derrida here was making a point he found himself obliged to repeat almost ad nauseam for the next twenty years) that deconstruction was in any sense reducible to Heidegger (*Po*, 73; 54). But neither was it the case that Heidegger's thought was itself reducible to his disastrous and far from negligible involvement with Nazism, which it was therefore important to examine, but not to the extent of censoring everything else. The irony was, at the very moment Derrida was being attacked by anti-Heideggerians for his interest in Heidegger, he was being rebuffed by faithful Heideggerians for his criticisms of his thought (*HF*, 100). And since one form of (politico-moral) resistance could always act as cover for another (philosophical) one, Derrida for his part made it plain in 1968 that he had no time for either camp: either the unconditional devotees or the unconditional enemies of Heidegger (*M*, 72; 62). It was necessary instead to take account of the indisputable advances of Heidegger and exercise at the same time the greatest possible rigour, a standpoint that Derrida was forced to reiterate (*PS*, 193–202; 181–91) when another so-called 'Heidegger affair' surfaced in 1987 following French publication of Victor Farias's polemical history of *Heidegger and Nazism*.

Derrida's relationship to Marxism was more complex. Deconstruction, he consistently argued, was inseparable from an articulation of political questions in the widest possible sense of the term. It was therefore impossible for it *not* to encounter Marx. This did not mean deconstruction could accept as given, as standard accounts of Marx tended to claim, that Marxian thinking was a homogeneous body of thought that had already overcome metaphysics. But this convergence between deconstruction and Marx, though undeniable, in the early 1970s, still belonged to the future, Derrida admitted (*Po*, 85; 63), not least because of the sheer complexity of the issues it raised. There was also the sentiment, Derrida observed subsequently, that there was no available place from which to begin that dialogue. To be critical of Marx in the 1960s and 1970s was to risk being painted as an anti-communist, which Derrida, for both philosophical and political reasons, was loath to see; equally, to endorse Marxism without reservation was not a viable solution either, all of which left Derrida stranded, reduced, so to speak, to silence on the issue, at least for the time being.

It was only in 1990, once the Berlin Wall had fallen, in much changed historical circumstances, that Derrida returned to the debate with Marxism, which resulted in the publication of *Specters of Marx*. To rekindle his interest in Marx at such a time invited the criticism of belatedness or inopportunity, which Derrida did not deny. What drove deconstruction, he explained, was not the attempt to destroy metaphysics, assuming this to be desirable or even possible, but what he described in the essay *Force of Law* as the indeconstructible demand for justice; and it was one of the hallmarks of any call for justice itself, he insisted, that it always fell at the wrong or inopportune moment, with an urgency that never could wait (*SM*, 144–5; 109–10). In that sense, there was no better time to evoke the ghosts of Marxism than at the precise moment when communism was being declared dead and buried on either side of the Wall. Deconstruction, Derrida argued, was always bound to countertemporality in this fashion, which did not prevent him throughout his career from adopting any number of firm political positions regarding philosophical institutions and other ethico-political issues, from the struggle against apartheid, racism, anti-semitism, censorship, and the death penalty to campaigning on behalf of so-called illegal immigrants, refugees, and others.

As regards psychoanalysis, and the theory of the psychoanalytic subject, things were again very different. In the 1971 interview with *Promesse*, Derrida enumerated his reservations with regard to the work of Lacan, which he developed more fully four years later, but which already bore essentially on Lacan's philosophical reprise of Freud, notably as far as the concept of the subject was concerned, explicitly taken from Hegel via Kojève, and including the famous triad of the Symbolic, the Imaginary, and the Real, also derived from Hegel (and Heidegger), and rearticulated on numerous occasions later. But though he could be critical of Lacan and of the work of other analysts, this did not prevent Derrida from having a nuanced and complex relationship with Freud's legacy, protective of its radical new thinking, but not incompatible with a readiness to abandon what he termed its residual positivism, not to mention significant elements in its initial conceptual edifice (*WT*, 279–86; 172–6).

Explaining his position to Elisabeth Roudinesco in 2001, at a time when Freudian psychoanalysis was under serious assault from the scientific and governmental establishment, he described his role as that of a friend of analysis, neither wholly inside nor properly outside, and able therefore to occupy in equal measure a place of both freedom and responsibility:

> 'The friend' is the one who approves, acquiesces, affirms the indelible
> necessity of psychoanalysis, that is, above all else, its future still to come
> [*son à-venir*], but the one who also takes an interest in the problematic,
> sometimes artificial, artefactual, and therefore deconstructible,
> perfectible character of the relationship between psychoanalysis and its
> law, like that between theory and practice, between the necessity of
> knowledge and its institutional inscription, between the public space of
> psychoanalysis and the absolute originality of its 'secret' space, which is
> irreducible to all 'publicity', beyond what is commonly acknowledged as
> legitimate under the heading of (medical or legal) 'professional secrecy'.
>
> (*WT*, 273; 168; translation modified)

A commitment to psychoanalysis, then, meant affirming the possibility and practice of analysis, without necessarily being satisfied with any aspect of its current institutions or received conceptual apparatus. Indeed, Derrida added, 'the "friend of psychoanalysis", in the face of so many metaphysical schemas at work in Freud's or Lacan's project, had to remain on his guard.' 'The gesture', he explained, 'was always double: it was to mark or remark a resource in Freud that had not yet been read, in my view, not in the way I believed it should, but at the same time to subject Freud the "text" (i.e., both theory and institution) to a deconstructive reading. Since no text is ever homogeneous . . ., it can be legitimate and is even always necessary to carry out a reading of it that is divided, differentiated, or even apparently contradictory' (*WT*, 278; 171; translation modified).

To read Derrida's three interviews from 1967, 1968, and 1971 collected in *Positions* is to discover a very different intellectual and ideological world to that with which most readers will be familiar today. It is striking nonetheless how many of the early objections raised in respect of Derrida's work – the relationship between philosophy, politics, and reason, the concept of history, the subject in psychoanalysis – did not disappear, but seemed to recur with regularity in the comments made by critics of Derrida in the years that followed. Time and again, he found himself obliged to explain his position with regard to Heidegger, Marx, Freud, and it was as though many of his most vociferous detractors not only failed repeatedly to read what he wrote, and respond to it as discussion demanded. It was no doubt also the case that it was in relation to ontology, history, and theories of subjectivity that deconstruction encountered its greatest resistance, not only in the sense that these were the issues deconstruction found most challenging, but also in that it was here critics found themselves most spectacularly unable to assimilate Derrida's thinking.

But the most prolonged, albeit strangely one-sided controversy involving Derrida and his English-speaking readers unfolded on yet another terrain: the theory of language. Here, too, what was oddly apparent was the inability of otherwise eminent critics properly to read Derrida and respond to his arguments in kind. 1976 was an important year for Derrida in the United States since it marked the publication of *Of Grammatology*, the first major work to be translated into English in its entirety. At around the same time Derrida had also begun teaching as a visitor at Yale. The following year, a new journal, *Glyph*, edited at Johns Hopkins by Samuel Weber and Henry Sussman, carried a translation of Derrida's 'Signature Event Context', publishing alongside it an extremely critical, not to say entirely dismissive 'Reply' by the leading speech-act theorist and philosopher, John R. Searle, who charged Derrida, among others, with confusing 'iterability' with what was merely 'the (relative) permanence of the written text over the spoken word'.[1] 'Derrida', Searle announced, 'has a distressing penchant for saying things that are obviously false',[2] and went on to take issue with Derrida's account of speech-act theory, arguing that 'Derrida's Austin is unrecognizable' and 'bears almost no relation to the original'.[3]

These were serious and potentially damaging assertions. It was hardly surprising, then, in the next issue of *Glyph*, Derrida replied in his turn. This he did at length and in detail, with both rigour and wit, and with a wealth of textual and other evidence, to devastating effect. There is not the room here to examine fully the exchange between Derrida and Searle. The main texts, with one exception, can now be consulted by readers in the volume *Limited Inc*, published in English in 1988 (a French edition followed two years later), which includes, in addition to Derrida's original essay and his 1977 reply to Searle, an extensive Afterword by Derrida, replying to questions provided by Gerald Graff, and examining once more the important stakes of the initial debate. Searle himself, however, was unwilling to have his original reply reprinted in the volume, and the reader has to make do with a summary of Searle's remarks supplied by Gerald Graff.

In retrospect, three aspects of the controversy are worth picking out. First, as Derrida is at pains to show, Searle's initial reading of 'Signature Event Context' was singularly deficient: superficial, muddled, and, in its own terms, somewhat incoherent. It failed properly to identify Derrida's arguments and respond to them as they deserved, to the point of formulating at times as objections arguments that Derrida himself had put forward. Second, one of the principal reasons for Searle's failure to understand Derrida's article was the difference in aim or purpose between the pair. Derrida's concern throughout, bearing just as much on Searle's misunderstanding as on the fact that performatives, too, can always fail, is to ask the question: 'How is all that possible? What does it imply?' (*L*, 63; 29). As Derrida maintains, any workable theory of performatives, as of most other things, must take proper account of what happens when things do not function as expected, intended, or wished, and integrate that possibility of failure within the theoretical model being articulated.

If this is not done, the theorist is left merely with norms, conventions, or assumptions, which, in the last resort, can only be imposed by recourse to prior dogmatic authority, which, as Derrida shows, is what is so powerfully undermines Searle's own position. Here a third aspect of Searle's discourse was apparent: his uncritical reliance on inherited binary concepts, which are not subjected to proper scrutiny by Searle, as they are by Derrida, and which include such crucial oppositions as that between use and mention, serious and non-serious, standard and non-standard, literal and metaphorical, fictional and non-fictional, ordinary and parasitic. Elsewhere, Searle attributes to Derrida the peculiar belief (peculiar, that is, from Searle's point of view) that 'unless a distinction can be made rigorous and precise it isn't really a distinction at all' (*L*, 207; 115). To which Derrida's riposte was uncompromising: it was that fuzzy concepts produced only fuzzy thinking, which ended up being inconsistent, confused, and dogmatic (*L*, 222–32; 123–8).

Such egregious failures of reading as those that characterise Searle's 'Reply' were not all. But as Derrida acquired a wider audience in the United States and elsewhere, so perceptions changed as to the precise theoretical framework and strategic import of his writing. Derrida, as he was read in the English-speaking world, was subtly different, and increasingly so, from the thinker who was an inhabitant of old francophone Europe. Admittedly, the two were not to remain separate for long, and there were in any case any number of complex reverse effects, as a result of which, as far as francophone and anglophone Europe was concerned, together with other countries too, what was identified as deconstruction was no longer something French, to the extent this had ever been the case, but more like an American import. All of this confused matters no end, and left the French, among others, increasingly suspicious of what had begun, so to speak, within their own shores. These numerous complex changes were no doubt inevitable, for precisely the reasons Derrida had articulated in 'Signature Event Context', but this did not mean they were necessarily always fruitful. If anything, they tended to accentuate the risk and prospect of misunderstandings.

The whole question of Derrida's engagement with so-called literary texts was a case in point. For two years after the exchange with Searle, Derrida, in English, contributed an essay, based on seminars he had been giving at Yale, to the volume entitled *Deconstruction and Criticism*. Despite the heterogeneity of its contributors, who shared an interest in philosophical perspectives on literature and were all employed at the time at the same institution, the book marked the arrival on the intellectual scene of something called the Yale School, which, for a short while at least, remained one of the most visible manifestations of deconstruction in America. In the Preface to the book, Geoffrey Hartman (who, oddly enough, signs in his own name while using the first-person plural 'we' throughout, only then to refer to himself in closing in the third person) wrote as follows:

> Deconstruction, as it has come to be called, refuses to identify the force
> of literature with any concept of embodied meaning and shows how
> deeply such logocentric or incarnationist perspectives have influenced
> the way we think about art. We assume that, by the miracle of art, the
> 'presence of the word' is equivalent to the presence of meaning. But the
> opposite can also be urged, that the word carries with it a certain
> absence or indeterminacy of meaning. Literary language foregrounds
> language itself as something not reducible to meaning: it opens as well as
> closes the disparity between symbol and idea, between written sign and
> assigned meaning.[4]

There was much here, no doubt, to which Derrida felt able to subscribe. Indeed, by publishing an essay of his own under the auspices of this presentational text, he may be deemed in part, if not to have co-authored it, to have at least co-signed or countersigned it. At the same time, it is plain that what Hartman proposes has relatively little to do with 'deconstruction' in the precise sense Derrida originally gave to the term. Any scrupulous reader of Derrida, for instance, might question the claim that there was a choice to be made between the presence of meaning or its absence or indeterminacy, which, from Derrida's perspective, are more like two derivative sides of the same faith in ontology, and far from what was implied by the thought of *différance*. Hartman's confident statement about the nature and identity of literary language, and the reliance on the concept of the written sign, were also problematic, and showed little evidence of even a cursory reading of *Of Grammatology*. And the idea that literature might still be understood as a foregrounding of language made it hard to resist the sense that what here was being presented as deconstruction was in fact a revamped version of New Criticism.

Hartman continued, 'The separation of philosophy from literary study has not worked to the benefit of either. Without the pressure of philosophy on literary texts, or the reciprocal pressure of literary analysis on philosophical writing, each discipline becomes impoverished' (p. viii). Many, including Derrida, will agree, at least up to a point. That point is however a crucial one. For it is hard to see from Derrida's perspective, for all the reasons explored in this book, how it might in fact be possible to subtract 'literary analysis' from philosophy, using it as a method of reading philosophy, even as philosophical methods themselves may be applied, unchanged, to reading literature. This was hardly what Derridian deconstruction had in mind. Hartman, though, was undiscouraged. 'If there is a danger of a confusion of realms', he added, 'it is a danger worth experiencing.'[5]

The danger was in fact far from negligible. It gave rise to a sequence of misunderstandings. For as deconstruction was better implanted in the United States and elsewhere, the belief became increasingly widespread that deconstruction, in a word, was the application of literary or aesthetic considerations to philosophical texts. Derrida, as a reader of philosophical writing, it was further alleged, was interested solely in word games. Writing in 1979 on Derrida's Hegel essay in *Glas*, the American philosopher Richard Rorty declared, for instance, that 'Derrida does not want to comprehend Hegel's books; he wants to play with Hegel. He doesn't want to write a book about the nature of language; he wants to play with the texts which other people have thought they were writing about language.'[6] Truth, argument, debate, others went on, none of this mattered much for deconstruction; aesthetic performance was all that counted. And if philosophy was suddenly found to be a branch of literature, all this proved was that there were no differences, that writing in Derrida's sense, as Rorty again has it, 'would be literature which was no longer opposed to philosophy, literature which subsumed and included philosophy, literature crowned king of an infinite undifferentiated textuality'.[7] No matter that none of this bore any resemblance whatsoever to what Derrida had actually written, it was easy enough to conclude from this point on that deconstruction was anti-philosophical aestheticism.

As far as Derrida was concerned, nothing could be further from the truth. First, there was nothing specifically literary about a concern for idiom, and what was often called literary or rhetorical readings rested on little more than an essentialist view of literature. Second, Derrida had no interest in effacing the difference between philosophy and literature. There was no truth in the claim sometimes attributed to Derrida that everything, because it was writing, was linguistic fabrication or fiction. True enough, Derrida challenged the authority with which philosophy, literary criticism, literary theory ordered their disciplinary boundaries. But the point was to accentuate differences, not dissolve them. There was no truth either in the claim that deconstruction was merely a form of textual hermeneutics, intent on cutting textuality adrift from the so-called outside world. The claims that Derrida was bent on destroying reason, neutralising politics, and turning everything into a closed literary game were absolutely without foundation.

Within a short space of time, many of these more bizarre assertions became a bandwagon to be leaped upon by conservatives or dogmatic progressives alike. In 1985, for instance, only two short years after having been elected overwhelmingly by fellow philosophers as the first Director of the newly created Collège international de philosophie, an important initiative the purpose of which was to develop a wide-ranging interdisciplinary forum for the exchange of philosophical ideas detached from state power and privilege, Derrida was being written off, once again, as a mere French derivative of Heidegger by Luc Ferry and Alain Renaut, two conservative French philosophers or ideologues, the former of whom, some years later, between 2002 and 2004, served under President Jacques Chirac as Minister of Education in Jean-Pierre Raffarin's right-wing government. Deconstruction, Ferry and Renaut charged, providing as evidence merely their own forced, superficial reading of certain texts by Derrida, was a project bent on eliminating reason, human will, and moral and ethical values, and turning theory into mere literature of no philosophical relevance. 'Derrida = Heidegger + Derrida's style', wrote Ferry and Renaut, revealing in their breathtaking obtuseness the dogmatic intolerance typical of their ideological position, even as they wondered, they said, 'what was left that was "French" in [Derrida's] astonishing enterprise of repetition'.[8] Inability to read, conformism, and xenophobia, not for the first time, nor probably the last, came here together as one.

Right-wing aggression of this kind was not all. From the 1960s onwards, Derrida's work prompted a vast amount of affirmative commentary too, in the writings of Nancy, Lacoue-Labarthe, Kofman, and numerous others, any complete account of which would fill a book much longer than this several times over. What this indicates most clearly of all perhaps, as is to be expected, is that the legacy of Derrida's own thought is divided, complex, interminable. Derrida spent much time in his work addressing the question of legacy. What then may be thought to be Derrida's own legacy? In the last interview he gave before his untimely death, which, when it was published, he sighed, already sounded too much like an obituary, he described in the following terms one of the crucial questions facing all who come after:

> Who is going to inherit, and how? Will there even be any heirs at all? The question is one that can be posed more than ever today. It is of constant concern to me. But the time of our techno-culture has radically changed in this respect. People of my 'generation', and of previous generations even more so, were used to a certain rhythm of history: we thought we could know whether such and such a work was capable of surviving or not, depending on its qualities, for one, two or even, as in the case of Plato, twenty-five centuries. Disappear, then be reborn. But today, the various accelerating modalities of archival storage, not to mention their deterioration or destruction, are transforming the structure and temporality, or the duration of heritage. For thinking itself, from this point on, the question of survival has begun to assume an absolutely unforeseeable shape. At my age, I am ready to accept the most contradictory hypotheses on the subject: I have simultaneously, please believe me when I say this, the *double sense* that, on the one hand, to put it with a smile and without any modesty, people have not yet even begun to read me, that, while there are, admittedly, many very good readers (ten, twenty, thirty or so, in the whole world, perhaps, people who are also writers as well as thinkers, and poets), basically it's only afterwards that everything will have a chance of becoming visible; but also, just as much, on the other hand, at one and the same time therefore, a fortnight or a month after my death, *there will be nothing left*. Except what is kept in a few copyright libraries. I swear it, I believe sincerely and simultaneously in these two hypotheses.    (*AV*, 34–5)

Everything, then, is in the texts and their multiple contexts, which are there for all to read.

## Further reading

In order to read Derrida on literature, to put it at its simplest, it is necessary to begin by reading.

But what?

Like any body of work of the breadth and magnitude of Derrida, there are foothills and mountains, steep escarpments and amenable plateaux, as well as a few bends in the river where it is possible to linger a while and enjoy the landscape. And as with any territory where the primary language spoken is not English, it is to be recommended that visitors acquire some knowledge of the local idiom or, if this is not possible, that they remember that at least something is always lost in translation and that, in reading Derrida, one is dealing with a writing that lends itself to translation *and* resists translation in almost equal measure.

All beginnings are difficult, said Marx, and there are many different tracks that can be followed in approaching Derrida. None are undemanding. At some stage, readers of Derrida will have to tackle *De la grammatologie*, that first major book of his that is rather oddly translated into English as *Of Grammatology*. This is however not an easy book, not least for reasons of length, which is why it is worth pausing after the first part of the book, 'Writing Before the Letter', in order to read, for instance, the first two, contemporaneous interviews collected in *Positions*, together with some of the essays in *Writing and Difference*, notably 'Freud and the Scene of Writing', 'Structure, Sign, and Play in the Discourse of the Human Sciences', 'La Parole soufflée' (on the poet and actor, Antonin Artaud), or 'From Restricted to General Economy', which deals with the novelist and essayist Georges Bataille.

At this stage, readers may go back to finish reading *Of Grammatology*. The hard (but exciting) work is not yet complete, for at this point it is a good idea to read 'Signature Event Context' in *Margins of Philosophy* together with the other texts relating to the controversy with Searle collected in *Limited Inc*. Readers can now envisage reading, with a greater sense of what is at stake, the essays on literary texts collected in *Acts of Literature*: on Mallarmé, Kafka, Blanchot, Joyce, Ponge, and Celan, supplemented with material from *Dissemination*, notably 'Outwork', 'Plato's Pharmacy' and the second of the two sessions on Mallarmé, and 'Le Facteur de la vérité' from *The Post Card*.

Few writers are as adept as Derrida at reinventing their thinking in response to new contexts, situations, or problems. There is always more Derrida worth reading. But such is the volume of Derrida's work that it is impossible to list everything here. Travellers are nonetheless recommended to consider equipping themselves with the following survival pack of texts, to be read selectively but closely and repeatedly:

*Of Grammatology*, corrected edition, translated by Gayatri Chakravorty Spivak, Baltimore, Johns Hopkins University Press (1976), 1997.

*Positions*, translated by Alan Bass, London, The Athlone Press, 1981.

*Writing and Difference*, translated by Alan Bass, London, Routledge, 1978.

*Margins of Philosophy*, translated by Alan Bass, Chicago, University of Chicago Press, 1982.

*Limited Inc*, edited by Gerald Graff, Evanston, Ill., Northwestern University Press, 1988.

*Acts of Literature*, edited by Derek Attridge, London, Routledge, 1992.

*Dissemination*, translated by Barbara Johnson, Chicago, University of Chicago Press, 1981.

*The Post Card*, translated by Alan Bass, Chicago, University of Chicago Press, 1987.

'Passions', in *On the Name*, edited by Thomas Dutoit, translated by David Wood, John P. Leavey, Jr, and Ian McLeod, Stanford, Stanford University Press, 1995.

There is a French proverb that states it is always better to address oneself to the good Lord than his Saints. So it is with Derrida too. But there are many illuminating articles and books about Derrida and literary matters that readers will find helpful. I list here, in alphabetical order, a number of works, some inevitably more demanding than others, that I have found useful in writing this book:

Geoffrey Bennington, *Jacques Derrida*, Chicago, University of Chicago Press, 1993. An informative and reliable account of Derrida's life and thought, with an important text by Derrida below.

*Interrupting Derrida*, London, Routledge, 2000.

Timothy Clark, *Derrida, Heidegger, Blanchot: Sources of Derrida's Notion and Practice of Literature*, Cambridge, Cambridge University Press, 1992.

John D. Caputo (ed.), *Deconstruction in a Nutshell: A Conversation with Jacques Derrida*, New York, Fordham University Press, 1997.

Tom Cohen (ed.), *Jacques Derrida and the Humanities: A Critical Reader*, Cambridge, Cambridge University Press, 2001.

Rodolphe Gasché, *The Tain of the Mirror: Derrida and the Philosophy of Reflection*, London, Harvard University Press, 1986. A demanding but always helpful philosophical account of Derrida.

*Inventions of Difference: On Jacques Derrida*, London, Harvard University Press, 1994. Contains the important essay 'Deconstruction as Criticism'.

Geoffrey H. Hartman, *Saving The Text: Literature/Derrida/Philosophy*, Baltimore, The Johns Hopkins Press, 1981. An influential though problematic discussion of *Glas*.

Joseph G. Kronick, *Derrida and the Future of Literature*, Albany, State University of New York Press, 1999.

Richard Rand (ed.), *Futures of Jacques Derrida*, Stanford, Stanford University Press, 2001.

Nicholas Royle, *Jacques Derrida*, London, Routledge, 2003. A wide-ranging introduction to Derrida's work.

# Notes

## 1 Life

1. For a detailed bibliography of Derrida's work, see the listing provided by Peter Krapp at www.hydra.umn.edu/derrida/jdyr.html.
2. These and other details regarding Derrida's life are drawn from the illustrated Curriculum vitae provided in Geoffrey Bennington and Jacques Derrida, *Jacques Derrida* (Paris, Seuil, 1991), 299–308; *Jacques Derrida*, translated by Geoffrey Bennington (Chicago, University of Chicago Press, 1993), 325–36. For the particular circumstances of Algerian Jews during the Occupation, see Michael R. Marrus and Robert O. Paxton, *Vichy France and the Jews* (Stanford, Stanford University Press [1981] 1995), 191–7.
3. See Michael R. Marrus and Robert O. Paxton, *Vichy France and the Jews*, 191. According to official figures, French North Africa as a whole (including Algeria, Morocco, and Tunisia), out of a total population of more that 13 million, contained 294,000 Jews.
4. See Michael R. Marrus and Robert O. Paxton, *Vichy France and the Jews*, 195.
5. Many of these speeches and texts are collected in Jacques Derrida, *Chaque fois unique, la fin du monde* (Paris, Galilée, 2003); *The Work of Mourning*, edited by Pascale-Anne Brault and Michael Naas (Chicago, Chicago University Press, 2001).
6. Jean Genet, *Journal du voleur* (Paris, Gallimard, 1949), 186; *The Thief's Journal*, translated by Bernard Frechtman (London, Anthony Blond, 1965), 156; translation slightly modified.
7. Borges offers a famous illustration of this paradox in the story 'Pierre Menard, Author of the *Quixote*', in *Labyrinths* (Harmondsworth, Penguin, 1970), 62–71.
8. Samuel Beckett, *Molloy, Malone Dies, The Unnamable* (London, John Calder, 1959), 418. Derrida felt very close to Beckett, he suggested to Derek Attridge (*A*, 60–2). On Beckett's reception by recent French philosophy, see my 'Poststructuralist Readings of Beckett', in *Palgrave Advances in Samuel Beckett Studies*, edited by Lois Oppenheim (London, Palgrave Macmillan, 2004), 68–88.
9. See *Pourquoi écrivez-vous?*, edited by Jean-François Fogel and Daniel Rondeau (Paris, Le Livre de poche, 1988), 232.

## 2 Contexts

1. Emmanuel Levinas, *En découvrant l'existence avec Husserl et Heidegger* (Paris, Vrin, 2001), 52–3; *Discovering Existence with Husserl*, translated by Richard A. Cohen and Michael B. Smith (Evanston, Ill., Northwestern University Press, 1998), 72–3.

2. See Simone de Beauvoir, *La Force de l'âge* (Paris, Gallimard, 1960), 141–2; *The Prime of Life*, translated by Peter Green (Harmondsworth, Penguin, 1965), 135–6. In her standard biography, Annie Cohen-Solal reports that, according to Aron, the trio were in fact drinking beer . . . See Annie Cohen-Solal, *Sartre 1905–1980* (Paris, Gallimard, 1985), 181–2.

3. See Jean-Paul Sartre, *Qu'est-ce que la littérature?* (Paris, Gallimard, 1948); *What is Literature?*, translated by Bernard Frechtman (London, Methuen, 1967).

4. A significant part of Blanchot's writing in the late 1940s is a sustained critique of Sartre's notion of committed literature ('littérature engagée'). See Maurice Blanchot, *La Part du feu* (Paris, Gallimard, 1949), 293–331; *The Work of Fire*, translated by Charlotte Mandell (Stanford, Stanford University Press, 1995), 300–44.

5. Ferdinand de Saussure, *Cours de linguistique générale*, edited by Tullio de Mauro (Paris, Payot, 1973), 166, author's emphasis; *Course in General Linguistics*, translated by Wade Baskin (New York, McGraw-Hill, 1966), 120.

6. See Ferdinand de Saussure, *Cours de linguistique générale*, 124–7; *Course in General Linguistics*, 87–9.

7. See Roman Jakobson, *Questions de poétique*, edited by Tzvetan Todorov (Paris, Seuil, 1973), 15. On the history of Russian Formalism and its legacy, see Victor Erlich, *Russian Formalism: History, Doctrine* (The Hague, Mouton, 1969), where the quotation from Jakobson is cited, p. 172.

8. Victor Shklovsky, 'Art as Technique', in *Russian Formalist Criticism*, edited and translated by Lee T. Lemon and Marion J. Reis (Lincoln, University of Nebraska Press, 1965), 12.

9. Victor Shklovsky, 'Sterne's *Tristram Shandy*', in *Russian Formalist Criticism*, 57.

10. See G. W. F. Hegel, *Werke*, edited by Eva Moldenhauer and Karl Markus Michel, 20 vols., Vol. VI (Frankfurt, Suhrkamp, 1970), 113–15; *Science of Logic*, translated by A. V. Miller (Atlantic Highlands, Humanities Press, 1989), 106–8; Miller translates the word as: *sublate*. Jean-Luc Nancy has devoted a whole book to Hegel's reliance on the double meaning of the word; see Jean-Luc Nancy, *La Remarque spéculative* (Paris, Galilée, 1973); *The Speculative Remark*, translated by Céline Surprenant (Stanford, Stanford University Press, 2001).

11. See Martin Heidegger, *Wegmarken* (Frankfurt, Klostermann, 1976), 313–64; *Basic Writings*, edited by David Farrell Krell (London, Routledge, 1993), 213–65. See too Martin Heidegger, 'Spiegel-Gespräch mit Martin Heidegger', in *Antwort: Heidegger in Gespräch*, edited by Günter Neske and Emil Kettering (Neske, Pfullingen, 1988), 107–8; 'Only a God Can Save Us', translated by Maria P. Alter and John D. Caputo, in *The Heidegger Controversy*, edited by Richard Wolin (Cambridge, Mass., MIT Press, 1993), 113; translation modified.

12. See Jacques Derrida, 'Forcener le subjectile', in Paule Thévenin and Jacques Derrida, *Antonin Artaud: Dessins et portraits* (Paris, Gallimard, 1986), 55–108; 'To Unsense the Subjectile', in *The Secret Art of Antonin Artaud*, translated by Mary Ann Caws (Cambridge, Mass., MIT Press, 1998), 60–157.

13. See Jacques Derrida, *Du droit à la philosophie* (Paris, Galilée, 1990); *Who's Afraid of Philosophy?: Right to Philosophy*, translated by Jan Plug (Stanford, Stanford University Press, 2002) and *Eyes of the University: Right to Philosophy 2*, translated by Jan Plug and others (Stanford, Stanford University Press, 2004); *L'Université sans condition* (Paris, Galilée, 2001); 'The University Without Condition', in *Without Alibi*, edited and translated by Peggy Kamuf (Stanford, Stanford University Press, 2002), 202–37.

14. *Plato's Phaedrus*, translated by R. Hackforth (Cambridge, Cambridge University Press, 1952), 158, 275e.

15. J. L. Austin, *How To Do Things With Words* (Oxford, The Clarendon Press [1962] 1975), 5.

16. J. L. Austin, *How To Do Things With Words*, 8; author's emphasis.

17. J. L. Austin, *How To Do Things With Words*, 9. In the following lecture Austin specifies six rules that must be observed if the performative is not to be 'unhappy' (14–24).

18. J. L. Austin, *How To Do Things With Words*, 22; author's emphasis.

## 3 Work

1. For an overview of the activities and influence of the Tel Quel group, see Patrick ffrench, *The Time of Theory: A History of Tel Quel (1960–1983)* (Oxford, Oxford University Press, 1995).

2. Stéphane Mallarmé, 'La Musique et les lettres', *Œuvres complètes*, edited by Bertrand Marchal, 2 vols. (Paris, Gallimard, 1998–2003), Vol. II, 65. Mallarmé does not refer here to 'literature' as such, as he does elsewhere, but to 'Letters [*les Lettres*]'. On Mallarmé's significance for twentieth-century French thought in general, see *Meetings with Mallarmé in Contemporary French Culture*, edited by Michael Temple (Exeter, University of Exeter Press, 1998).

3. Maurice Blanchot, *L'Espace littéraire* (Paris, Gallimard, 1955), 35; *The Space of Literature*, translated by Ann Smock (Lincoln, Nebr. and London, University of Nebraska Press, 1982), 42–3; translation modified. Blanchot's words echo a famous remark by Heidegger in *An Introduction to Metaphysics*, translated by Ralph Manheim (New Haven, Yale University Press, 1959), 32.

4. Stéphane Mallarmé, *Œuvres complètes*, II, 108.

5. Stéphane Mallarmé, *Œuvres complètes*, II, 217.

6. See Jean-Luc Nancy, *L'Intrus* (Paris, Galilée, 2000); 'L'Intrus', translated by Susan Hanson, *The New Centennial Review*, 2, 3 (2002), 1–14. Derrida writes at length about identity trouble in Nancy's work in *Le Toucher, Jean-Luc Nancy* (Paris, Galilée,

2000); *On Touching – Jean-Luc Nancy*, translated by Christine Irizarry (Stanford, Stanford University Press, 2005). The film director Claire Denis based her 2004 film *L'Intrus* (*The Intruder*) on Nancy's story.

7. See Sigmund Freud, *On Sexuality*, edited by Angela Richards, translated under the editorship of James Strachey, The Pelican Freud Library, Vol. VII (Harmondsworth, Penguin, 1977), 351–7.

8. Sigmund Freud, *On Sexuality*, 356; translation modified.

9. Jean-Pierre Richard, *L'Univers imaginaire de Mallarmé* (Paris, Seuil, 1961).

10. For a detailed exploration of the poetic thinking at work in the poem, see Roger Pearson, *Unfolding Mallarmé* (Oxford, Oxford University Press, 1996), 233–92.

11. See Stéphane Mallarmé, *Œuvres complètes*, I, 231–346. On Mallarmé's fan-poems, see Roger Pearson, *Mallarmé and Circumstance* (Oxford, Oxford University Press, 2004), 194–207.

12. On reflexivity in Derrida, see Rodolphe Gasché, *The Tain of the Mirror: Derrida and the Philosophy of Reflection* (Cambridge, Mass., Harvard University Press, 1986).

13. See Roland Barthes, *S/Z* (Paris, Seuil, 1970); *S/Z*, translated by Richard Miller (London, Jonathan Cape, 1975). Miller translates the two terms problematically, in my view, as *readerly* and *writerly* respectively.

14. I have done so elsewhere, in my *Radical Indecision: Barthes, Blanchot, Derrida, and the Future of Criticism*, forthcoming.

15. Maurice Blanchot, *Le Pas au-delà* (Paris, Gallimard, 1973); *The Step Not Beyond*, translated by Lycette Nelson (Albany, State University of New York Press, 1992).

16. Blanchot's *L'Arrêt de mort* (*Death Sentence*), together with *La Folie du jour* (*The Madness of the Day*), and other fictional writings and essays, may be found in English in *The Station Hill Blanchot Reader*, edited by George Quasha, translated by Lydia Davis, Paul Auster, and Robert Lamberton (Barrytown, Station Hill Press, 1998). For an overview of Blanchot's work, see my *Blanchot: Extreme Contemporary* (London, Routledge, 1997).

17. See Jacques Derrida, *Donner le temps 1. La fausse monnaie* (Paris, Galilée, 1991); *Given Time: 1. Counterfeit Money*, translated by Peggy Kamuf (Chicago, University of Chicago Press, 1992). The previous year, Blanchot had published a tribute to Derrida of his own: 'Grâce (soit rendue) à Jacques Derrida', *Revue philosophique*, 2 (April–June 1990), 167–73; 'Thanks (Be Given) to Jacques Derrida', translated by Leslie Hill, *The Blanchot Reader*, edited by Michael Holland (Oxford, Blackwell, 1995), 317–23.

18. See Maurice Blanchot and Jacques Derrida, *The Instant of My Death / Demeure: Fiction and Testimony*, translated by Elizabeth Rottenberg (Stanford, Stanford University Press, 2000).

19. See Jacques Derrida, *Chaque fois unique, la fin du monde*, edited by Pascale-Anne Brault and Michael Naas (Paris, Galilée, 2003), 323–32. This funeral homage to Blanchot postdates the English edition of *The Work of Mourning* and is included only in the French version of the book.

20. In *La Contre-allée*, Derrida describes himself as standing somewhere between Heidegger and Blanchot, each of whom represented, in very different ways, he suggests, a kind of 'implacable prosecutor and counter-model' (*C*, 25; 17). Blanchot was also a more than usually astute reader of Heidegger, as I suggest in *Blanchot: Extreme Contemporary*, 77–91, and in 'A Fragmentary Demand', in *The Power of Contestation: Perspectives on Maurice Blanchot*, edited by Kevin Hart and Geoffrey H. Hartman (Baltimore, Johns Hopkins University Press, 2004), 101–20.

21. See Philippe Lacoue-Labarthe and Jean-Luc Nancy, *L'Absolu littéraire* (Paris, Seuil, 1978); *The Literary Absolute*, translated by Philip Barnard and Cheryl Lester (Albany, State University of New York Press, 1988). Unfortunately the English translation contains only the authors' introduction and commentary.

22. Friedrich Schlegel, *Dialogue on Poetry and Literary Aphorisms*, translated by Ernst Behler and Roman Struc (London, Pennsylvania State University Press, 1968), 140.

23. See Gérard Genette, *Introduction à l'architexte* (Paris, Seuil, 1979); *The Architext: An Introduction*, translated by Jane E. Lewin (Berkeley, University of California Press, 1992).

24. Maurice Blanchot, *La Folie du jour* (Paris, Gallimard, 2002), 9; *The Station Hill Blanchot Reader*, 191; translation modified.

25. Maurice Blanchot, *La Folie du jour*, 17; *The Station Hill Blanchot Reader*, 194; translation modified.

26. Maurice Blanchot, *La Folie du jour*, 30; *The Station Hill Blanchot Reader*, 199; translation modified.

27. Maurice Blanchot, *La Folie du jour*, 9, 29; *The Station Hill Blanchot Reader*, 191, 199; translation modified.

28. See Maurice Blanchot, *Le Pas au-delà*, 41; *The Step Not Beyond*, 27.

29. Maurice Blanchot, *La Folie du jour*, 24; *The Station Hill Blanchot Reader*, 197; translation modified.

30. Maurice Blanchot, *La Folie du jour*, 18–19; *The Station Hill Blanchot Reader*, 194–5; translation modified.

31. Marie Bonaparte, *The Life and Works of Edgar Allan Poe: A Psychoanalytic Interpretation*, translated by John Rodker (London, The Hogarth Press, 1949), xi.

32. For a compendium of texts relating to Lacan's account of Poe, including the 1957 essay together with material by Bonaparte, Derrida, and numerous others, see *The Purloined Poe: Lacan, Derrida, and Psychoanalytic Reading*, edited by John P. Muller and William J. Richardson (Baltimore, The Johns Hopkins University Press, 1988). For an accessible guide to Lacan's often difficult work, see Malcolm Bowie, *Jacques Lacan* (London, Fontana, 1991); and Jean-Michel Rabaté, *Jacques Lacan* (Houndmills, Palgrave, 2001). On the often turbulent history of psychoanalytic institutions in France, see Elisabeth Roudinesco, *La Bataille de cent ans: Histoire de la psychanalyse en France*, 2 vols., Vol. II: 1925–1985 (Paris, Seuil, 1986); *Jacques Lacan & Co: A History of Psychoanalysis in France, 1925–1985*, translated by Jeffrey Mehlman (Chicago, University of Chicago Press, 1990).

33. Edgar Allan Poe, *The Complete Tales and Poems* (Harmondsworth, Penguin, 1982), 220; *The Purloined Poe*, 21.

34. Jacques Lacan, *Ecrits* (Paris, Seuil, 1966), 12; 'Seminar on "The Purloined Letter"', translated by Jeffrey Mehlman, *The Purloined Poe*, 29; translation slightly modified.

35. Jacques Lacan, *Ecrits*, 15; *The Purloined Poe*, 32; translation modified.

36. Jacques Lacan, *Ecrits*, 30; *The Purloined Poe*, 43–4; translation modified.

37. On the whole question of psychosis in Lacan, see *Ecrits*, 531–83; *Ecrits: A Selection*, translated by Alan Sheridan (London, Tavistock Publications, 1977), 179–225. It is here that the legacy of Kojève's anthropological reading of Hegel is particularly in evidence. Readers here might also turn to Gilles Deleuze and Félix Guattari's *L'Anti-Œdipe* (Paris, Minuit, 1972); *Anti-Oedipus*, translated by Robert Hurley, Mark Seem, and Helen R. Lane (London, Athlone, 1984), a book as profoundly indebted to Lacan's thought as it is fiercely hostile to it.

38. Marie Bonaparte, *The Life and Works of Edgar Allan Poe*, 483; *The Purloined Poe*, 130.

39. For an exposition of this kind of 'delayed action', 'deferred effect' or *Nachträglichkeit* in Freud, see the article on 'Après-Coup' or 'Deferred Action' in Jean Laplanche and J.-B. Pontalis, *Vocabulaire de la psychanalyse* (Paris, P. U. F., 1997), 33–6; *The Language of Psychoanalysis*, translated by Donald Nicholson-Smith (London, The Hogarth Press, 1973), 111–14. For more detailed discussion of Derrida's dual evaluation of Freud's work, see Geoffrey Bennington, *Interrupting Derrida* (London, Routledge, 2000), 93–109.

40. See Nicolas Abraham and Maria Torok, *Cryptonymie: Le Verbier de l'homme aux loups* (Paris, Aubier-Flammarion, 1976); *The Wolf Man's Magic Word: A Cryptonomy*, translated by Nicholas Rand (Minneapolis, University of Minnesota Press, 1986). Derrida wrote again on Abraham's work for American readers in 1979 in 'Me – Psychoanalysis: An Introduction to the Translation of "The Shell and the Kernel" by Nicolas Abraham', *Diacritics*, 9,1 (1979), 4–12. The original French appears as 'Moi – la psychanalyse' in *Psyché* (*Psy*, 145–58).

41. Sigmund Freud, *Case Histories II*, edited by Angela Richards, translated under the editorship of James Strachey, The Penguin Freud Library, Vol. 9, (Harmondsworth, Penguin, 1979), 218.

42. Sigmund Freud, *The Interpretation of Dreams*, edited by Angela Richards, translated under the editorship of James Strachey, The Penguin Freud Library, Vol. 4 (Harmondsworth, Penguin, 1976), 363.

43. Sigmund Freud, *The Interpretation of Dreams*, 342.

44. I borrow the misdirected jibe, which occurs in the context of a discussion of the work of Alain Badiou, from Slavoj Žižek in *The Ticklish Subject* (London, Verso, 2000), 131.

45. Compare Jacques Lacan, *Ecrits*, 12–13; *The Purloined Poe*, 30. On the Freudian primal scene (or *Urszene*), see Jean Laplanche and J.-B. Pontalis, *Vocabulaire de la psychanalyse*, 432–3; *The Language of Psychoanalysis*, 335–6.

46. See Maurice Blanchot, *L'Entretien infini* (Paris, Gallimard, 1969), 556–67; *The Infinite Conversation*, translated by Susan Hanson (Minneapolis, University of Minnesota Press, 1993), 379–87. I discuss the essay in more detail in my *Bataille, Klossowski, Blanchot* (Oxford, Oxford University Press, 2001), 206–26.

47. Maurice Blanchot, *L'Entretien infini*, 565–6; *The Infinite Conversation*, 386; translation modified.

48. Edgar Allan Poe, *The Complete Tales and Poems*, 208, 217; *The Purloined Poe*, 6, 17. 'The Purloined Letter' is not the only text in which Lacan is keen to map out triangles in this way. He adopts a similar approach in another, less well-known essay, one of only a few he published on a specific literary text, his 1965 review of Marguerite Duras's novel, *Le Ravissement de Lol V. Stein* (*The Ravishing of Lol V. Stein*), now in Jacques Lacan, *Autres écrits* (Paris, Seuil, 2001), 191–7, and, in an English translation by Peter Connor, in *Duras on Duras* (San Francisco, City Lights Books, 1987), 122–9. I discuss Lacan's reading of Duras in more detail in my 'Lacan with Duras', in *Writing and Psychoanalysis: A Reader*, edited by John Lechte (London, Edward Arnold, 1996), 143–66. For an alternative perspective, see Jean-Michel Rabaté, *Jacques Lacan*, 115–34.

49. See Sigmund Freud, *Art and Literature*, edited by Albert Dickson, The Penguin Freud Library, Vol. XIV (Harmondsworth, Penguin, 1985), 339–76.

50. Jacques Lacan, *Ecrits*, 11; *The Purloined Poe*, 29.

51. Jacques Lacan, *Ecrits*, 41; *The Purloined Poe*, 53; translation slightly modified.

52. Slavoj Žižek, *Enjoy Your Symptom!* (Routledge, London, revised edition 2001), 10; author's emphasis throughout.

53. Compare the discussion of Lacan's treatment of the difference between animals and humans in Jacques Derrida, *L'Animal que donc je suis* (Paris, Galilée, 2006), 163–91; 'And Say the Animal Responded?', translated by David Wills, in *Zoontologies: the Question of the Animal*, edited by Cary Wolfe (Minneapolis, University of Minnesota Press, 2003), 121–46.

54. Jacques Lacan, *Le Séminaire, Livre XXIII: Le Sinthome (1975–6)*, edited by Jacques-Alain Miller (Paris, Seuil, 2005), 144. On Lacan's Joyce, see Jean-Michel Rabaté, *Jacques Lacan*, 154–82, where Rabaté quotes a slightly different version of the remark (p. 176). In mathematics, Borromean rings consist of three circles which are linked together as a trio, despite the fact that no two of them are linked together. If one link is removed, all three are released.

55. James Joyce, *Finnegans Wake* (London, Faber & Faber, 1964), 120.

56. James Joyce, *A Portrait of the Artist As A Young Man* (Harmondsworth, Penguin, 1966), 215.

57. James Joyce, *Finnegans Wake*, 170.

58. James Joyce, *Ulysses*, edited by Declan Kiberd (Harmondsworth, Penguin, 1992), 498. Derrida quotes this passage in *UG*, 132; *A*, 302.

59. James Joyce, *Ulysses*, 269.

60. James Joyce, *Finnegans Wake*, 175.

61. James Joyce, *Finnegans Wake*, 120.

62. James Joyce, *Ulysses*, 498.

63. James Joyce, *Finnegans Wake*, 258.

64. Samuel Beckett, *Malone meurt* (Paris, Minuit, 1951), 115; Samuel Beckett, *Molloy, Malone Dies, The Unnamable*, 236.

65. Franz Kafka, *Gesammelte Werke*, edited by Hans-Gerd Koch, 12 vols., Vol. III (Frankfurt, Fischer, 1994), 230; *The Trial*, translated by Breon Mitchell (New York, Schocken Books, 1998), 220.

66. See Paul de Man, *The Resistance to Theory* (Minneapolis, University of Minnesota Press, 1986).

67. Juliette's celebrated dictum appears in the closing pages of the *Histoire de Juliette*; see Sade, *Œuvres*, edited by Michel Delon in collaboration with Jean Deprun, 3 vols., Vol. III (Paris, Gallimard, 1990–98), 1261. It is quoted by Blanchot in *La Part du feu*, 311; *The Work of Fire*, 321.

## 4 Reception and further reading

1. John R. Searle, 'Reiterating the Differences: A Reply to Derrida', *Glyph*, 1 (1977), 200.

2. John R. Searle, 'Reiterating the Differences', 203.

3. John R. Searle, 'Reiterating the Differences', 204.

4. Harold Bloom et al., *Deconstruction and Criticism* (London, Routledge and Kegan Paul, 1979), vii–viii.

5. Harold Bloom et al., *Deconstruction and Criticism*, ix.

6. Richard Rorty, *Consequences of Pragmatism (Essays 1972–1980)* (Minneapolis, University of Minnesota Press, 1982), 96.

7. Richard Rorty, *Essays on Heidegger and Others* (Cambridge, Cambridge University Press, 1991), 92.

8. Luc Ferry and Alain Renaut, *La Pensée 68* (Paris, Gallimard, 1985), 167, 168.

# Index